TH᷑
SEATON ᴸ ᴴ
AND
SEATON TRAMWAY
by
Colin G. Maggs

Mouth of River Axe, Seaton, Devon.

THE OAKWOOD PRESS

© Oakwood Press 1992

ISBN 0 85361 425 3

Typeset by Gem Publishing Company, Brightwell, Wallingford, Oxfordshire.

Printed by Alpha Print (Oxon) Ltd, Witney, Oxon.

Acknowledgements

Grateful acknowledgement for assistance is due to: P.E. Barnes; C. Chivers; W.G. Clarke; A.J.V. Gardner of Seaton & District Electric Tramways; F.G. George; R.A. Lumber; G.T. Reardon; D.R. Steggles and A.E. West.

Special thanks must go to P.K. Tunks who assisted with the section on timetables and Dr T.R.N. Edwards who checked the manuscript.

Photographed on July 9th, 1945; this view of Seaton shows the locomotive shed (*left*) and the gasworks roof (*right*) behind the stone yard of the Beer Stone Company. Class 0415, 4–4–2T No. 3488 awaits the 'off' with the 10.10 am, Saturday through coaches to Waterloo.   *H.C. Casserley*

Published by
The OAKWOOD PRESS
P.O.Box 122, Headington, Oxford.

On 5th August, 1933 the up 'Atlantic Coast Express', sporting 12 coaches, headed by 'King Arthur' class 4−6−0 No. 749 *Iseult* roars down Honiton bank on the through line. The Seaton branch curves left behind the signal box.   *S.W. Baker*

Contents

Bibliography

Allen, G.F.; *The Southern Since 1948*; Ian Allan 1987.

Boyle, V.C. & Payne, D.; *Devon Harbours*; Christopher Johnson 1952.

Bradley, D.L.; *LSWR Locomotives: The Adams Classes*; Wild Swan 1985.

Bradley, D.L.; *LSWR Locomotives: The Drummond Classes*; Wild Swan 1986.

Bradshaw's Railway Manual, Shareholders' Guide & Directory, 1869.

Clinker, C.R.; *Closed Stations & Goods Depots*; Avon-Anglia 1978.

Hateley, R.; *Industrial Locomotives of South West England*; Industrial Railway Society 1977.

Hawkins, C. & Reeve, G.; *An Historical Survey of Southern Sheds*; OPC 1979.

Pryer, G.A.; *Track Layout Diagrams of the Southern Railway & BR SR, Section 5*; R.A. Cooke 1982.

Seaton & Beer Railway Company Minute Books. RAIL 601. 1–2. Public Record Office.

Seaton Tramway; Seaton Tramway, no date.

Seaton Tramway; Jarrold Colour Publications 1986.

Veal, C. & Goodman, J.; *Auto Trains & Steam Rail Motors of the Great Western*; Great Western Society 1981.

Williams, R.A.; *The London & South Western Railway*; Volumes 1 & 2, David & Charles 1968 & 1973.

Newspapers and Magazines: *Exeter Flying Post*; *Express & Echo*; *Western Morning News*; *Railway Magazine*; *Trains Illustrated*.

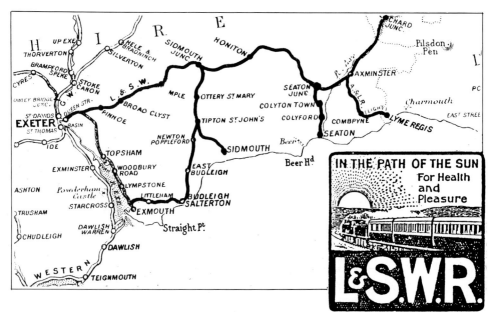

Introduction

The easternmost resort on the Devon coast, with a population of 4,974 (1981), Seaton lies on the western side of the wide valley through which the River Axe flows to the sea. It was known to the Phoenicians before the Roman settlement of Moridunum was made nearby. The Danes used the area for their marauding campaigns, and it was mentioned in Domesday as Fluta. In 1347 the inhabitants supplied and crewed two ships to aid the Siege of Calais, but by the reign of Henry VIII the erosive action of the River Axe and the tides had built a pebble ridge at the mouth of the river, effectively blocking the entrance to anything larger than fishing vessels. Subsequent attempts to remove the ridge met with no success, and the economy began to suffer.

In the 19th century the topography of the district did not lend itself to a railway following the coast, while in any case, such a line would have been rather off the shortest route from London to Exeter. The circumstances suggested that the best policy was to build a branch line from the London & South Western Railway which had been opened to Exeter in 1860. The Seaton branch opened on 16th March, 1868 and served the district well, causing the town to change its character from port to resort. The Southern Railway carried out modernisation of the branch and junction station, but then in the 1960s, with so many people travelling by road in their own vehicles, it became uneconomic to keep the line open and it succumbed to the axe in 1966. However, the route had a scenic value and an electric tramway was opened along the greater part of the track formation; this concern is still flourishing today and adds to the tourist attractions of the area.

Population of Seaton

1801	1871	1891	1911	1931	1951	1961	1971	1981
1,497	2,155	2,339	1,694*	2,349	2,903	3,410	4,139	4,974

*This decrease is inexplicable.

A general view of Seaton Junction; looking 'up' shows the main lines (*left*) and the Seaton branch (*right*). The nearest concrete footbridge carries a public path over the line.   *Lens of Sutton*

'West Country' 4–6–2 No. 34030 *Watersmeet* leaves with the 2.37 pm to Exeter. Ex-GWR '64XX' class 0–6–0PT No. 6412 waits with the branch train to Seaton on 26th October, 1963.

E. Wilmshurst

Chapter One
The Seaton & Beer Railway: 1863–1887

The first railway scheme to involve Seaton was the Axminster, Seaton & Beer Junction Railway, put forward in 1861 with Henry Conybeare as Engineer. In spite of its name, it was only planned to run from the London & South Western Railway at Colyton to Seaton, but the plan also involved building a road bridge across the River Axe at Seaton. This particular scheme failed on Standing Orders, but an Act (26–7 Vic. cap. 118) was passed for constructing a very similar railway, also with a road bridge, and this received Royal Assent on 13th July, 1863. A capital of £36,000 was authorised in £10 shares and £12,000 on loan. Arrangements were made with the LSWR to work the line for 45 per cent of receipts.

The first meeting of the Seaton & Beer Railway, as the company was finally called, was held at the Pole Arms Inn, Seaton on 5th December, 1863. Sir Walter Calverley Trevelyan, lord of the manor of Seaton, was elected Chairman of the Board of Directors; Richard Maynard, Secretary; William Robert Galbraith, Engineer; and Messrs Radcliffe & Davies, solicitors. Significantly, Galbraith was also Engineer to the LSWR. On 8th January, 1864 a contract was signed with Howard Ashton Holden, London, for constructing the line. At the meeting on 27th August, 1864 it was reported that the contractor had started work and staked out the line from end to end. The Board of Trade sanctioned a slight deviation, as the SBR wished to run the railway along Seaton Marsh Bank by widening it on the east, instead of the west side as originally proposed, the modification effecting a considerable saving in expense of both land and works.

In February 1865 little progress could be reported. Notices to treat for purchase of land had been served on all landowners and an agreement had been made on 2nd January with Sir John Pole, through whose land the line was to run for two miles, for it to be purchased at £120 per acre. At Seaton the embankment along the foreshore of the River Axe was completed for nearly a mile, but no progress took place on any other sections of the line. Complaints were made to James H. Shipway, the contractor's agent, who said that the severe weather had affected the money market and prevented more vigorous action on the civil engineering side; Holden promised to proceed with the works rapidly 'as soon as the weather has fairly set in.'

On 28th April the solicitors and Secretary were directed to give notice to the contractor 'that unless on or before 30th June next he completes the works pursuant to Article 15 of his contract, the Directors will rescind and put an end to the contract and take such other steps as counsel may advise'. William Miller then entered into partnership with Holden and on 2nd June, 1865 a supplemental contract was signed with Holden & Miller.

By August the contractors were in possession of nearly four miles of line but were doing very little construction. Galbraith expressed dissatisfaction with progress and believed it impossible to complete the works by 1st January, 1866, the extended time limit fixed by the supplementary contract, and advised that unless steps were taken at once, the summer traffic of 1866 would be lost. Shipway was therefore informed that unless active proceedings were taken within a fortnight, the contract would be terminated.

Three weeks later, Holden & Miller had made no progress. It was found that they lacked the necessary finance, despite the fact that Sir Walter Trevelyan, the SBR's Chairman had provided the contractor with a considerable sum as well as taking nearly half the shares. Therefore the contract was finally terminated on 27th September, 1865. John Sampson worked on the line from 29th September, and a contract was signed with him on 10th October, 1865 at which point he promised that within 10 days of acceptance he would place 20 earth wagons and 25 tons of temporary rail on the ground as plant. Eleven days later, Radcliffe found Sampson had no wagons or temporary way, and had made no arrangements for the purchase of rails and sleepers, wishfully thinking he could get them on credit.

At a meeting on 4th November it was announced that the Railway Finance Company would be prepared to furnish Holden & Miller with funds, but if the Directors were unable to wait a fortnight, Shipway (the contractor's agent) said he would take over the contract himself. He played for time, but failed to satisfy the Directors regarding his financial scheme and so was dropped. On 30th November, Holden's solicitor, G.E. Gastard, wrote saying that as the railway company threatened to let his client's contract, he would at once file a Bill and apply for an injunction against the SBR. The Directors replied that they were willing to consider any proposals that Holden & Miller might make within a month.

Pending negotiations relating to the re-letting of the contract to a suitable applicant, Sampson continued with the works. With at least three-quarters of it still to be executed, a contract was signed on 17th February, 1866 for William Shrimpton to complete it for £26,500, made up of £8,000 cash, £13,500 in five per cent debenture shares and £5,000 in ordinary shares. Then, just when everything appeared settled, Shrimpton declined to proceed on the grounds that Holden had threatened proceedings if he did so. Attempts were made to re-let the contract, but pending negotiations Sampson continued with the works. A contract was negotiated on 2nd June, 1866 with him for £12,000 preference stock and £22,890 ordinary shares, Sir Walter Trevelyan agreeing to purchase the shares and preference stock for £10,000 cash on completion of the contract. Sampson agreed to complete the works on or before 1st March, 1867. Bird & Co. tendered for the supply of 500 tons of rails at £6 10s. 0d. per ton, exclusive of carriage, while William Wheaton of Exeter's tender for 6,500 half-round sleepers at 2s. 10½d. each and 2,300 rectangular sleepers at 3s. each, was accepted.

Meanwhile the SBR realised it had insufficient funds to complete the line, and on 18th April, 1866 the Board of Trade issued a certificate for raising an additional capital of £12,000 in five per cent preference shares and £4,000 on loan.

At the half-yearly meeting on 8th February, 1867 it was announced that Sampson had failed to make the progress which by his contract he was bound to make, but the SBR still hoped the line would be ready for traffic during the course of the summer and appealed to landowners and others to take up the mortgage debentures.

Seaton LSWR station c.1910. Notice the short rail lengths and the lack of run-round facilities. Posters advertise the delights of Ilfracombe, Paris, Southsea and Swanage whilst the station staff pose for their photograph during a lull in the traffic!
Lens of Sutton

A pictorial aerial view of the station area from the east side of the River Axe showing the holiday camp beyond, dated August 1942. *Author's collection*

Completion of the bridges was delayed as Kerslake of Exeter refused to deliver tie rods, bolts and other materials unless the SBR guaranteed £30. In February a locomotive was required for assisting with the work of making the line, but the one promised to Galbraith (the Engineer) could not be delivered until April since it required repair. Sampson himself was unable to procure an engine as he had no money for its hire. As there was insufficient horse power to carry out the works, Sampson was instructed to use a further six horses which would do rather more than the work of a locomotive at a nearly similar price.

That Galbraith showed compassion to Sampson is known in his letter to the Directors on 8th March. 'Mr [James] Muir [the SBR manager] should be empowered to advance to Sampson a weekly allowance for his own use. I do not see how this is to be avoided if the semblance of keeping Sampson on is to be retained, for he has neither money nor credit and without some provision the man will starve.' This appeal resulted in the Board voting Sampson £2 weekly.

On 8th June it was resolved that a locomotive would be hired from Isaac Watt Boulton's Engineering Works, Ashton-under-Lyne to assist with the works as soon as the bridge across the Colyton turnpike was completed: this was certainly running by 2nd August.

On 5th July, 1867 a contract was signed with Birmingham & Co. of Broad Clyst for building the three stations for a total of £6,700 and a level crossing cottage at Colyford for £525, the cost of these being deducted from Sampson's contract. Messrs Birmingham were required to do some smart work, as 1st September was the completion date for the booking offices and goods sheds, the station masters' houses to be completed a month later, as it was hoped that the opening of the line would take place on 1st October. The same firm also built the timber engine shed at Seaton for £200. By 2nd August a locomotive hired from Boulton was at work allowing six horses to be dispensed with.

On 2nd August Galbraith reported that the bulk of the earthworks was finished, but widening and raising of the embankments was required, while slopes needed to be trimmed and soiled, but he said that, if necessary, this could be completed after the railway was opened. Masonry and culverts were nearly complete and 2½ of the 4¼ miles ballasted. The Electric Telegraph Company had fixed their installations along the line for £150. Water for station and engine purposes at Seaton was to have been bought from a Mr Hallett for £10 a year, the railway laying a 3 in. pipe under the river for £50, but he insisted on limiting the supply to 1,000 gallons daily and refused any for station use at Seaton. This resulted in the treaty with him being abandoned, and a supply from Sir Walter Trevelyan's estate obtained at £10 a year.

Some interesting sidelights on branch line operating are cast by reports of an altercation between the SBR and the LSWR. On 17th December, 1866, Frederick Clarke, Secretary of the LSWR criticised the working terms proposed by the SBR, which were that the LSWR would work and maintain the line at 45 per cent of gross receipts and that the £800 annual interest of the debenture debt would be the first charge on these receipts. He would not

Seaton Junction, looking in the 'down' direction c.1910, in the days long before the track was quadrupled.   *Author's collection*

An up train hauled by a 4–4–0 pauses at Seaton Junction. This 1927 picture shows reconstruction into a four-track station in progress as the new down platform can be seen left of the footbridge.   *S.W. Baker*

admit the latter, and said that his company would work and maintain the line for 60 per cent of gross receipts. On 17th January, 1867 he modified the proposal, saying that the LSWR would take 60 per cent of gross receipts until the receipts reached £12 per mile/week when the expenses would be reduced to 50 per cent. Trevelyan appealed to the LSWR Directors as he believed that as the landowners had built the line at their expense, the LSWR should be more helpful. On 8th March, 1867 the LSWR agreed on 55 per cent of the gross receipts in perpetuity.

This offer was not immediately accepted, as the SBR wished to calculate the expense of working the line itself but found that no builders were prepared to lend rolling stock. One company even refused to entertain an order for so small a number of vehicles and the SBR found that deferred payment over five years could bring the cost of a £285 coach up to £370. It would have been quite uneconomic for the SBR to have owned a sufficient variety of wagons to deal with goods traffic, and these would need to have been hired from the LSWR.

Galbraith, Engineer to the SBR, assessed that traffic could be dealt with by a tank engine, a first and second class composite coach, a third class coach and guard's van, the cost of these being about £1,850. He estimated the annual running expenses:

Traffic	....	....	....	....	....	£650 0s. 0d.[1]
Locomotive	....	....	....	....	....	£625 0s. 0d.[2]
Permanent way	....	....	....	....	....	£245 0s. 0d.
Management	....	....	....	....	....	£150 0s. 0d.
Interest on plant	....	....	....	....	....	£92 10s. 0d.
						£1,762 10s. 0d.

The length of the line was 4¼ miles, which enabled the LSWR to charge for five miles, and Galbraith found that if the gross earnings amounted to £10 per mile/week, the figures would be:

Yearly income of	....	....	....	....	....	£2,600
Less 55 per cent for working		....	....	....	....	£1,430
Net income if worked by LSWR			....	....	....	£1,170

while if the SBR worked the line itself:

Gross traffic	....	....	....	....	....	£2,600 0s. 0d.
Less working expenses		....	....	....	....	£1,762 10s. 0d.
Net income	....	....	....	....	....	£837 10s. 0d.

the balance in favour of LSWR working being a substantial £332 10s. 0d. In addition, no allowance had been made for repairs and renewals of rolling

---

1. Had the SBR worked the line, the wages of the station masters, porters and guards would have totalled £550 per annum plus £100 for stores.
2. Locomotive department wages would have been £209 a year, and fuel and other items £8 per week.

stock, and no provision was made for hiring a locomotive when repairs were needed. The only additional expense to the SBR, if worked by the LSWR, was the cost of station masters' houses at Colyton and Seaton which did not amount to over £600.

A further factor in favour of having the line worked by the LSWR was that if the SBR worked the line itself and an accident occurred, the revenue for many years could be swallowed up by one compensation case. The Directors therefore resolved that the LSWR terms for working should be accepted and the agreement was signed on 31st December, 1867.

The anticipated October opening proved too optimistic an estimate, but early December found the line almost complete, the Board of Trade being notified that the railway would be ready for inspection by 20th December. Colonel Yolland, inspected the line on 27th December and reported to the Secretary of the Board of Trade, as follows:

Sir,

I have the honor [sic] to state for the information of the Board of Trade that in obedience to your minute of the 13th Instant, I yesterday inspected the Seaton and Beer Railway, which commences at Colyton Station of the Yeovil and Exeter Branch of the London and South Western Railway and ends at Seaton, a length of 4 miles and 30½ chains.

This Line is single throughout, and no provision has been made, either in land or works, for a double Line.

The width of the Line at formation Level is 18 ft, the gauge is 4 ft 8½ inches and the width between Sidings and main Line is 6 ft.

The permanent way consists of a flat-bottomed rail that weighs 65 lb. per linear yard in lengths mostly of 24 ft, placed on transverse sleepers laid at an average distance of 3 ft apart. No chairs are made use of, but the rails are fastened to the sleepers by a fang bolt on the inside and a spike on the outside of each rail. The joints of the rail are fished with two plates together weighing 17 lb. and 4 bolts and nuts together weighing 5 lb.

The sleepers are either of larch or of fir creosoted 9 ft long, by 9 in. × 4½ in. scantling (half round).

The ballast consists of flint gravel and of shingle from the seashore at Seaton, stated to be 1 foot deep.

There are 10 under bridges and 3 Viaducts. The largest span has an opening of 41½ ft on the skew – and this under bridge has Stone abutments and wrought iron girders. One of the Viaducts of 33 ft span is similarly constructed. Two other bridges have stone abutments and cast-iron girders and the remainder are constructed with brick or stone abutments and Timber beams – or altogether of Timber. All the iron girders are sufficiently strong by calculation and exhibited moderate deflections under a rolling load.

The steepest gradient is 1 in 76.7 and the sharpest curve has a radius of 15 chains. Stations have been constructed at Colyton, Colyford and Seaton.

There are no authorised Level Crossings of Public Roads on the Line.

In making my inspection I noticed the following:

1. It is proposed to make use of the down Platform of the London and South Wn Station at Colyton Jn for the Seaton and Beer Trains – but to do this, as at present constructed, it is necessary to shunt the Trains with Passengers in the Carriages, whether going in or coming out from the Station, for a distance of about 200 yards. This is very objectionable. It would be more desirable to construct a platform

'O2' class 0−4−4T No. 187 about to leave Seaton. Note the apparatus on the engine for air-controlled motor-train operation. The concrete River Axe road bridge is on the left; 5th August, 1933. *S.W. Baker*

'M7' class 0−4−4T No. 30046, (shedded at 72A, Exmouth Junction) stands at the branch platform Seaton Junction, with a push-pull train for the branch. A crowd waits on the up main line platform for the mainline service. *Lens of Sutton*

alongside of the line adjacent to the Colyton Jn Station – with shelter for the Passengers on it. The Bank at the west end of this station is not properly consolidated.

2. The Signal arrangements at Colyton Jn Station were not complete and the locking apparatus did not prevent contradictory signals from being given. A low signal is also required to prevent Trains from coming out from the goods yard, north of the London and South Western lines, and fouling both lines of way. This signal should interlock with the main line signals – and this through road should lead into a blind siding north of the loop line when this signal is at danger and be locked by it in that position.

3. At Colyton Station, the down distant Signal when taken off to admit a down train should lock the points open for the main line. Buffer stops are required at the end of the Goods Siding.

4. At Colyford Station the Platform is too short, it should be lengthened by at least 50 feet.

5. The Platforms of the bridges which are constructed with wrought or cast-iron girders, should have longitudinal beams laid on them to carry the rails, with cross transomes and strap bolts to keep the gauge correct.

5. [Yolland repeats this number in error. CGM] A good deal of the Fencing is of wire, with posts at 9 ft apart – where this is the case, intermediate posts are required – the wires in many parts also want tightening up – and there are openings below the lowest wires that should be stopped up.

6. Where the Ballast is wholly of shingle, some additional gravel ballast is required to make it bind properly.

7. Many of the check rails at the crossings at the Junction Station and at Seaton Station are not placed at the proper distance from the rails. This should be attend. [sic]

8. Clocks that can be seen from the Platforms are required at all the Stations.

I have not received the undertaking, as to the mode of working the line, but I understand it is to be worked by the London and South Western Ry Co and by one Engine in Steam.

I have now therefore to report, that, by reason of the incompleteness of the works, the opening of the Seaton & Beer Railway for Traffic, cannot be sanctioned without danger to the Public using the same.

In due course Sir Walter Trevelyan sought an interview with the President of the Board of Trade and was told that if on re-inspection everything else was satisfactory, the line could be opened on the undertaking (signed 2nd March, 1868), that a platform at the Junction would be built within six months of one being required. Re-inspection was carried out on 19th February, 1868, with Yolland submitting the following report to the BoT:

Sir,
I have the honor to state for the information of the Board of Trade, that in obedience to your minutes of the 11th Instant, I have re-inspected the Seaton & Beer Railway, and to report that the whole of my requirements have been attended to, with the exception of the first and sixth.

With respect to the first, I still think the Board of Trade should require the construction of a Platform with Shelter on it, adjacent to this new Line at Colyton Junction Station, allowing the Company time to comply with the requirement, in accordance with the decision of the President and Vice President on the 30th Ultimate, but giving notice at once – otherwise the Seaton & Beer Railway Co. may be called upon by the London & South Western Railway Co. to erect the Shelter they have stipulated for on the Down Platform – and the ground between the two Lines may be occupied by sidings rendering the construction of the new Platform and pathway to the London & South Western Station more difficult. Neither do I see how the Inspecting Officers can require shunting to be avoided in future on other Lines, unless provision is made in this instance when it can be done at so little expense.

As regards the Ballast, more care and attention will require to be given to the maintenance of the Line, where the shingle only is used.

There are some small portions of Marsh between the Railway and the River Axe near Seaton, which are not fenced off from the Railway. I was told that these would not be stocked, and I did not ask for the fencing to be done, in consequence of such a statement.

It must however be distinctly understood that this fencing will require to be done, before these Marshes are stocked and this understanding should I think be embodied in one of the undertakings from the Railway Company.

I have not received any undertakings as regards the mode of working the Traffic, or the construction of a Platform at the Colyton Junction. When these are received and are deemed satisfactory, the sanction of the Board of Trade may be given to the opening for traffic.

On 27th February, 1868 Captain Charles E. Mangles, Chairman of the LSWR, sent a letter to the SBR requiring it to set aside money so that the wooden engine shed and platform at Seaton, platform walls at Colyford and the two timber bridges could be replaced and also transverse wrought iron girders inserted in two other bridges. The SBR Directors were shocked at the thought of this additional expense, and sought arbitration from the President of the Institution of Civil Engineers. To satisfy the LSWR, during the following month the SBR gave an undertaking that it would reinstate the structures with durable materials. A year later, Charles Hutton Gregory, giving judgment on 15th March, 1869, said that the SBR was properly constructed, but remarked that the company should rebuild with brick, stone or iron the all-timber bridge north of Colyford, but that he was satisfied with the timber bridge to the south. The northern bridge was anticipated to last 14 years from the opening of the line and a replacement would cost £220. Gregory required a covered way to be constructed at Seaton between the booking office and the platform waiting shed.

The line was opened on 16th March, 1868. There was no public celebration, but many inhabitants of the neighbourhood travelled on the line that day. N.R. Gillingham of Shute was appointed superintendent at £1 per week until 16th March, 1869, his job entailing supervising the workmen and making up the pay sheets.

On 31st July the Engineer, Galbraith, walked over the line and found the permanent way and works in excellent order, only a little ballast being required to make up one embankment where it had subsided. On 18th September Gillingham said that eight men were required to keep the line in good repair and it could not be kept in order at less cost. He observed that the embankment at the junction required widening immediately.

A very early view of Seaton before the holiday camp was built. Note the stone yard on the right. The River Axe road bridge can be seen in the middle foreground.

Courtesy H.M.R.S.

Seaton c.1910, showing the station building with station master's house beyond. The shorter passenger platform is to the right whilst the main platform (*left*) proved to be also too short and was extended soon after opening. A goods van stands at buffers at the end of the loading dock. *Lens of Sutton*

Traffic for the half year ending 30th June, 1868 was:

Coaching receipts	....	....	....	....	....	£300 7s. 3d.
Goods receipts	....	....	....	....	....	£43 12s. 11d.
						£344 0s. 2d.
Government duty	....	....	....	£8 16s. 11d.		
Working expenses @ 55 per cent	....	....	....	£189 4s. 1d.		
						£198 1s. 0d.
				Income		£145 19s. 2d.

The number of passengers booking from Colyton Town and Seaton between 16th March and 30th June, 1868 was:

	1st single	2nd	3rd	1st ret.	2nd	3rd	Total
Colyton Town	112	2,054	3,569	47	666	39	6,487
Seaton	365	2,369	4,165	299	1,231	1,786	10,215

Frederick Clarke, LSWR Secretary, wrote on 28th July, 1869 saying that in accordance with the agreement dated 31st December, 1867, Seaton platform should be extended northward for 180 ft to enable it to cope with excursion traffic. Galbraith suggested to the SBR Directors that, as the extension of the platform was only required for excursion traffic, they could defer replying to the LSWR for a week and then say that as the summer was passing, the matter could be left until the spring – a neat way of delaying matters! Lengthening was carried out in the following spring, at a cost of £60 3s. 0d., provided by the Chairman as a further loan to the company.

The LSWR was anxious for the line to have 'improving touches'. In 1872 it installed a five ton crane at Seaton, but pressed the SBR to provide a water tank at Colyton the following year; also in September 1874 the LSWR Secretary wrote asking for an enlargement of the office at Colyton Town station, which was found to be inadequate. The SBR Directors claimed their company was not liable as the existing office had been accepted by the LSWR, and its enlargement would not have been an undertaking the SBR would have carried out had they been working the line themselves. However, the LSWR made the alterations they required and sent the SBR a bill for £39 9s. 11d. In December 1875 the LSWR required further accommodation at Colyford station, but the SBR declined making the outlay, saying it was only a level crossing cottage with a ticket office and platform for the benefit of the neighbourhood. Persons requiring better accommodation could use Colyton or Seaton stations only a mile distant. The Directors anticipated that when the Axmouth Bridge had been constructed, traffic at Colyford was likely to decrease, as much of it would be transferred to Seaton station.

In the original Act, it had been planned to throw a bridge across the Axe from Seaton station to ease access from Axmouth and Rousdon. Six hundred and fifty pounds had been paid to Hallett in August for the site of the bridge and ferry tolls, but lack of cash prevented the project being carried out until an extraordinary meeting on 8th December, 1875 authorised the Directors to raise up to £3,000 by the creation of 'Axmouth Bridge Stock'. A contract with William Jackson, Westminster, for building the bridge was signed on 15th December, 1875. Philip Brannon was Engineer to the bridge undertaking.

Colonel Yolland inspected the completed structure on 18th April, 1877. It consisted of a central arch having a 50 ft span and two side arches of 30 ft span over the main stream of the river and tideway, while one of about 15 ft span on the skew crossed the swatchway. An unusual feature was that the whole of the bridge and toll house was built in concrete. The toll house, situated 100 yds west of the bridge, is reputed to be the oldest concrete house in England. A toll of 4d. was charged for each horse and cart crossing the bridge, a penny a leg for animals in harness and a halfpenny a leg for those not in harness. The story runs that one miserly farmer unharnessed his horse at one end of the bridge and made his son pull the cart across! The bridge was opened to public traffic on 24th April, 1877, the staff of Seaton station being allowed to cross toll free.

On 28th February, 1877 Trevelyan retired from the Board and Henry Ellis, Deputy Chairman, was appointed in his place. He only held office for two years and, at his death, was replaced (on 27th August, 1878) by Trevelyan, who had rejoined the Board, but not for long as he also died. Early in the following year, George Evans was appointed to the Chair, on 27th February, 1880. The Secretary, C.E. Rowcliffe, died on 3rd May, 1877 and Edwin Hellard, successor to his practice at Stogumber, was appointed on 16th June, 1877.

The SBR Directors, dissatisfied with the receipts forwarded by the LSWR, passed a resolution on 31st August, 1876 that the LSWR accounts relating to the working agreement of the Seaton branch be examined. H. Cecil Newton, of the Buckfastleigh, Totnes & South Devon Railway carried out this inspection and found that the LSWR used the following principle in preparing its accounts (*the figures examined by Newton may be seen in Appendix One*):

For through coaching traffic, embracing passenger, parcels, excursion and livestock, the Seaton & Beer only received a mileage proportion of the through charge. This was in accordance with Railway Clearing House practice except as regards passenger traffic on which Newton considered that the SBR should be credited with the full local fare before division. For purely local traffic on the line, the whole receipts were put in the joint purse and divided under the agreement, but the greater part of the passenger traffic was, of course, through traffic.

Regarding goods and mineral traffic to and from places on the LSWR, that company treated it as 'local traffic', that is, it did not recognise the independence of the SBR and credited it with a mileage proportion only, the SBR receiving nothing for the expense of providing a terminal. The LSWR claimed that this was in accordance with the agreement, but Newton was of the opinion that the agreement was never intended to bear that construction, for its effect was to 'practically ruin' the SBR as its traffic was sent principally to the LSWR system and that system alone. For goods and mineral traffic to and from places beyond the LSWR, terminal allowances were credited to the SBR, the terminal on coal traffic being 6d. a ton which the SBR accepted.

Newton wrote: 'From my examination of the accounts I have no reason to doubt their accuracy so far as the South Western Company is concerned, but not as regards the Seaton and Beer line for if the construction put upon the agreement by the South Western Company be the right one, (which I altogether doubt), I do not think it possible financially speaking, for the Seaton and Beer Company to exist.'

Regarding mails and advertisements, the SBR proportion was only a mileage one. Newton considered that the company should have been paid a lump sum. 'In my judgement the Seaton and Beer Company has a substantial claim against the South Western, which I think might be enforced by an application to the Railway Commissioners, though an amicable settlement would be more satisfactory.' The only terminals* allowed to the SBR were on 'foreign' coal traffic, but the Railway Clearing House credited the LSWR with all the 'terminals' and Newton believed that the LSWR should have, in turn, credited the SBR for the money so received. If the LSWR had allowed a 'terminal' on traffic to the LSWR, the SBR would have received approximately an additional £178 for the six months ending 31st December, 1876.

Newton said that the average yield per ton was about 9d. compared with 1s. 7d. on the Buckfastleigh Railway. The number of passengers carried during the same period was approximately 34,000, with an average receipt of 3d per passenger compared with 6d. on the Buckfastleigh Railway. Pressure from the SBR Directors persuaded the LSWR to make a reasonable and proper charge for wharfage accommodation at stations, not only on the SBR, but on the whole of the LSWR.

On 28th February, 1879 the SBR resolved to sound out the LSWR and the Great Western Railway to find out what terms it would offer for the purchase of the line. The terms of Archibald Scott, LSWR Traffic Manager, were that his company would take out a thousand year lease for £1,000 per annum, increasing by annual instalments of £100 to £1,500, and in the following year rising £50 to a sum of £1,550 per annum in perpetuity. This would have provided an income of 4 per cent on debentures and the arrears of debentures; 3 per cent on preference shares and one per cent on ordinary shares.

The LSWR had the option of purchasing the company by issuing to debenture holders and shareholders a sufficient quantity of its 4 per cent preference stock, to meet the respective dividends and on receipt of such stock, the SBR would be extinguished.

The LSWR had no wish to be responsible for the bridge over the Axe, as if the company bought it, the neighbourhood would probably have agitated for it to be set free from toll. The SBR Board agreed to these tentative terms and arranged for the Axmouth Bridge to go to Sir Alfred Trevelyan of Nettlecombe, Somerset, who inherited Sir Walter's estate. On 27th August, 1881 the deed of transfer and the conveyance of the bridge undertaking were signed and sealed and £3,000 ordinary stock authorised by the SBR (Axmouth Bridge Certificate) for shares, cancelled. In 1907, Sanders Stephens, owner of the manor, had the bridge made toll free.

Meanwhile the LSWR (Various Powers) Act (43—44 Vic. cap. 183) received Royal Assent on 26th August, 1880. Under this Act and the agree-

---

*Terminals – allowance for providing terminal facilities to handle goods traffic such as sidings, goods shed, weighbridge and manpower.

ment dated 27th November, 1879, the LSWR agreed to exercise its option to pay in cash, the transfer to take place as from 1st January, 1888. The LSWR paid off the debenture holders to the amount of their principal, namely £15,200 and £5,057 2s. 4d. arrears of interest. Preference shareholders received 75 per cent of the nominal amount of their stock, ordinary shareholders receiving £2 per share.

Cash capital for division		£17,782 17s. 8d.
75% of £12,000 preference stock	£9,000	
£2 per share of 3600 ordinary shares	£7,200	
	£16,200	£16,200 0s. 0d.
	Leaving a balance of	£1,582 17s. 8d.

The conveyance of the SBR to the LSWR was duly completed on 3rd January, 1888.

'K10' class 4–4–0 No. 384 (with smoke box wing plates and six-wheel tender), approaching Seaton Junction on 6th August, 1934 with a return Bank Holiday excursion comprising nine six-wheeled coaches, believed to be ex-SECR stock. *S.W. Baker*

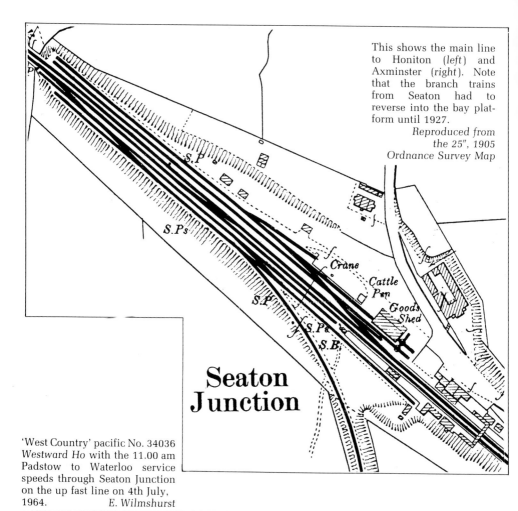

This shows the main line to Honiton (*left*) and Axminster (*right*). Note that the branch trains from Seaton had to reverse into the bay platform until 1927.

Reproduced from the 25″, 1905 Ordnance Survey Map

S.P

S.Ps

Crane

Cattle Pen

Goods Shed

S.P

S.Ps

S.B.

Seaton Junction

'West Country' pacific No. 34036 *Westward Ho* with the 11.00 am Padstow to Waterloo service speeds through Seaton Junction on the up fast line on 4th July, 1964.   E. Wilmshurst

THE RAILWAY EXECUTIVE
PASSENGERS
MUST NOT CROSS
THE LINE HERE

Chapter Two

Subsequent History and Description of the Line

The line flourished under LSWR and Southern Railway control and even as late as August 1959, 3,500 tickets were issued and 12,000 collected at Seaton, quite apart from passengers using Holiday Runabout season tickets. On a summer Saturday in 1964 about 1,200 passengers used the station, over 200 of these being clients of Warner's Holiday Camp. Despite this traffic the Beeching Report recommended closure. On 1st January, 1963 the branch was transferred from the Southern to the Western Region. Seaton and Colyton Town were closed to goods traffic on 3rd February, 1964, the latter station becoming unstaffed on that date. The branch closed completely on 7th March, 1966 with less than a dozen passengers making the last trip. Seaton Junction on the main line also closed to passengers on this date and became a coal depot only from 18th April, 1966. The former milk depot sidings there were taken out of use in June 1973.

Seaton Junction

Colyton for Seaton, 147 m. 63 ch. from Waterloo, was opened on 18th July, 1860 as a single line station on the main LSWR line to Exeter. With the opening of the branch on 16th March, 1868, the station was renamed Colyton Junction, but to avoid confusion with Colyton station, became Seaton Junction in July 1869. The actual junction faced Exeter and was at the west end of the station, which meant that trains had to reverse either in or out of the bay at the down end of the down platform until a platform (No. 3) was built on the sharp curve of the branch line before the junction. This work, carried out by the SR, was opened on 13th February, 1927.

The whole station was modified at this time with through running lines being provided and platform loops, the main line platforms being considerably lengthened. Until the through roads were built, there was no place where an express could overtake a stopping train on the 49 miles between Yeovil Junction and Exeter. The new layout, costing £46,000, was opened on 3rd April, 1928, the platform walls, overbridges and sign boards being in the reinforced concrete style adopted by the SR.

The new signal box, which opened on the same date, contained a 55-lever frame. The tall, co-acting up starting signals were unusual in that they differed from normal practice which was for the lower arms to follow the same priority as the upper ones. Although the upper arm for the through line was higher than that for the platform loop, both lower arms were at the same height.

A borehole was sunk to over 280 ft, but supplied no more than 90 gallons per hour which was obtained at 34 ft! In 1935 additional water for the station and adjacent dairy ran via a 3 inch diameter pipe from Honiton Tunnel, five miles away. The first milk train left the plant during the second week of September 1934 in one tank, a GWR 6-wheeler branded 'West Park Dairy Co Ltd' of 3,000 gallons capacity, but only two-thirds full. The Express

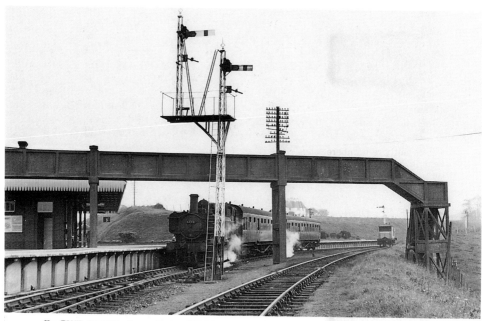

Ex-GWR '64XX' class, 0–6–0PT No. 6412 seen here on 26th October, 1963 at the branch platform (No. 3). The signals had to be 'lofty' in order not to be obscured by the concrete footbridge which carried a public path across the whole station complex.

E. Wilmshurst

Ex-GWR '14XX' class 0–4–2T No. 1450 in a poor state heading auto-coach W240W on the Branch service on 12th February, 1965.

A.E. West

The recently re-numbered 'M7' class 0−4−4T No. 30105 shunts milk tank wagons at Seaton Junction on 18th July, 1948. Locking bars can be seen on the up main and up through roads to prevent points from being moved when a vehicle was on that portion of track.   *A.E. West*

Ex-LBSCR 'D1' class 0−4−2T, No. B256 and gated saloons (probably Set 373) at the branch platform, Seaton Junction in the early nineteen-thirties.   *Author's Collection*

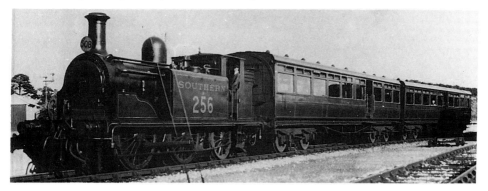

An Adams radial tank engine No. 30583 having just shunted the 'through' Seaton to Waterloo coach on to the up train standing at the platform, waits for the up express, hauled by 'Merchant Navy' No. 35009 *Shaw Savill*, to pass before re-crossing all the main tracks back to the branch line on the left. Photographed on 16th September, 1950.   *S.W. Baker*

'O2' class 0−4−4T No. 183 drifts in with the branch train on 29th May, 1936. The through Seaton to Waterloo coach is behind the locomotive, with the branch coaches trailing. To the left of the large advertisement hoarding stand the up and down main line trains awaiting the exchange of passengers to and from Seaton. The up through coach will be shunted on to the rear of the up train whose engine may be seen just above the left hand poster board. No. 183 is festooned with gear for the air-controlled motor-train operation.   *S.W. Baker*

'M7' class 0−4−4T No. 30048 with push and pull set No. 1, seen on 9th December, 1961 in the branch platform at Seaton Junction.   *A.E. West*

Seaton Junction looking towards Honiton on 2nd September, 1959 with the 3.34 pm ex-Templecombe service departing with No. 30827 in charge. The Seaton branch platform is on the left. *H.B. Priestley*

Seaton Junction signal box as seen on 9th July, 1949. Note the branch line push-pull set on the extreme right. The branch platform is beyond the signal box on the left. *H.C. Casserley*

A Gloucester Railway Carriage & Wagon Company single unit DMU, awaits its next run to Seaton on the branch service.   *Lens of Sutton*

An Exeter slow train leaves Seaton Junction with 'King Arthur' No. 30449 *Sir Torre* piloting 'S15' class No. 30827. The Seaton branch is on the left; 16th September, 1950.   *S.W. Baker*

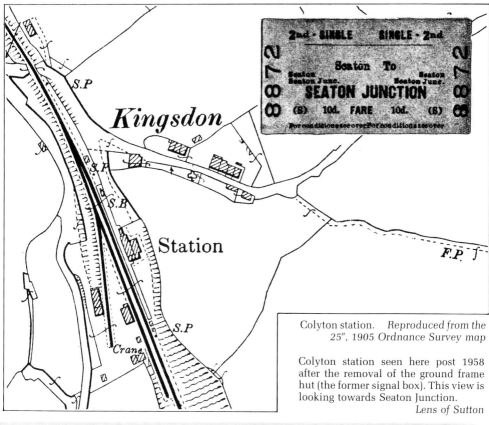

Colyton station.   *Reproduced from the 25", 1905 Ordnance Survey map*

Colyton station seen here post 1958 after the removal of the ground frame hut (the former signal box). This view is looking towards Seaton Junction.

Lens of Sutton

Dairy Co. took over on 1st October, 1934 and new contracts brought in about 4,000 gallons, so one tank was despatched and the surplus sent in churns. The original goods shed was converted into a milk cooling station.

After the station's closure, the main line was singled on 11th June, 1967, and in October 1972 the former down through road, which had been in use until that date, was slewed over to the site of the former up through road. The station building of brick construction still stands, and is notable for its unusually wide multiple chimney stacks. This building and the former dairy are now occupied by the Axminster Engineering & Moulding Company.

Colyton

The branch line descended at 1 in 100 for over a mile, steepening to 1 in 76 before Colyton (1 m. 64 ch.). Named Colyton Town until September 1890, the station had a single passenger platform situated on the east side of the line across the river from the village, and necessitated a road journey of about half a mile. The station building is vaguely Italianate in design and although generally of red brick, it is banded by yellow and black bricks, the round headed windows also having this pattern. The building is now a tea room. The station was unstaffed from 19th May, 1964. A water tank was situated at the down end of the platform. There was a goods shed and two sidings which faced down trains.

The signal box opened on 5th March, 1899, when the system of working changed from the train staff to Tyer's train tablet, the new signal box

A view west of Colyton station with the picturesque village beyond the River Coly. In the goods yard stand private owners' wagons, open wagons with LSWR branded tarpaulins and an LSWR meat van. This view shows well the substantial station buildings and goodshed.   *Author's Collection*

The Westinghouse signal ground frame at Colyton station on 4th May, 1959.   *A.E. West*

'Barley sugar' pattern gas lamp standard and fire buckets at Colyton station seen on 4th May, 1959.   *A.E. West*

The small goods shed/store at the up end of the passenger platform at Colyton station seen here 26th September, 1964.   *A.E. West*

A view of Colyton station buildings showing the double sliding doors to the ticket office. Note the changing brick colour for the arch windows. *A.E. West*

BR Standard class '3MT' 2−6−2T No. 82040 deputising for a dmu at Colyton station on 26th September, 1964. *A.E. West*

Colyton station with 'M7' class 0-4-4T No. 49 hauling Motor set No. 723 as the 2.45 pm Seaton to Seaton Junction service on 28th June, 1948. The third class brake coach nearest the camera is S3855 and the destination label in the rack bears the words 'Seaton Branch'.

J.H. Aston

'M7' class 0-4-4T No. 30048 with up train pauses at Colyton to pick up or set down a van.

Lens of Sutton

S.W. Baker

A fine view of Colyton station on 30th May, 1936, looking towards Seaton.

On 2nd June, 1959 at Colyton station No. 30021 is seen leaving with motor set No. 381 for Seaton Junction with the 2.05 pm service. Note the goods shed canopy has now been removed and the water tank obtained a roof whilst the station roof has received repairs!   *J.H. Aston*

Ex-GWR '64XX' class 0−6−0PT No. 6412 waits with the 2.20 pm Seaton to Seaton Junction service on 26th October, 1963. The indicator on the water tank shows that it is empty.   *E. Wilmshurst*

A fine detailed view of the water tank at the southern end of Colyton station, 4th May, 1959. Notice the gauge outside the tank, and the hand pump, above which is a small cast notice 'Not Drinking Water'.   A.E. West

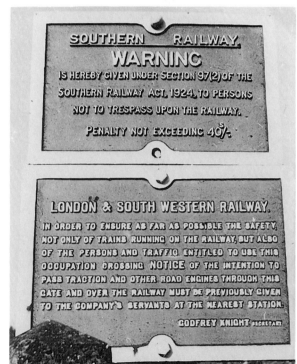

SOUTHERN RAILWAY.
WARNING
IS HEREBY GIVEN UNDER SECTION 97(2) OF THE
SOUTHERN RAILWAY ACT, 1924, TO PERSONS
NOT TO TRESPASS UPON THE RAILWAY.
PENALTY NOT EXCEEDING 40/-

LONDON & SOUTH WESTERN RAILWAY.
IN ORDER TO ENSURE AS FAR AS POSSIBLE THE SAFETY,
NOT ONLY OF TRAINS RUNNING ON THE RAILWAY, BUT ALSO
OF THE PERSONS AND TRAFFIC ENTITLED TO USE THIS
OCCUPATION CROSSING NOTICE OF THE INTENTION TO
PASS TRACTION AND OTHER ROAD ENGINES THROUGH THIS
GATE AND OVER THE RAILWAY MUST BE PREVIOUSLY GIVEN
TO THE COMPANY'S SERVANTS AT THE NEAREST STATION.
GODFREY KNIGHT SECRETARY

Cast iron notices at Colyford station, 24th September, 1964.
A.E. West

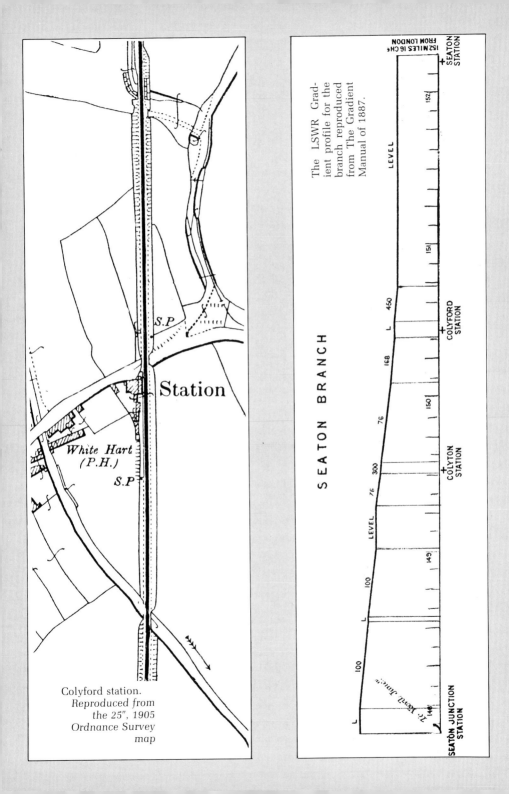

Colyford station.
Reproduced from
the 25", 1905
Ordnance Survey
map

Station

White Hart
(P.H.)

S.P

S.P

SEATON BRANCH

The LSWR Grad-
ient profile for the
branch reproduced
from The Gradient
Manual of 1887.

152½ MILES 16 CH⁹
FROM LONDON

SEATON
STATION

LEVEL

450 L

168

76

300 76

LEVEL

100

100 L

COLYFORD
STATION

COLYTON
STATION

To Axm. Junc.

SEATON JUNCTION
STATION

A general view of Colyford station and level crossing on 2nd June, 1965. *J.P. Alsop*

Colyford looking north, on 1st June, 1936. Note cast iron gentlemen's urinal, still in use. The two rows of fire buckets beyond were necessary to protect the timber-built booking hall and waiting rooms. Note the platform has been lengthened at some stage, the extension having a brick, instead of concrete, facing. *S.W. Baker*

breaking the previous block section into two. For most of the year, the signals displayed large crosses as the box was only switched in for the summer peak. At such times the Seaton Junction – Seaton tablets were locked away at the junction and a fresh set to cover the two sections was released from storage by a key held at Exeter and brought into use.

The 1921 *Appendix to the Rules, Regulations and Working Timetables* stated that the points worked by the signal box were controlled by the train tablet, the signalman being required to send a 'Release Tablet for Shunting' signal to the next tablet station, and, having obtained permission, then to withdraw a tablet from his Tyer's No. 6 instrument. When shunting was completed, the tablet was required to be replaced and the appropriate signal sent.

On 4th April, 1922 the signal box was reduced to a ground frame released by the train tablet. It closed on 4th November, 1958 when a new ground frame was opened at the north end of the complex. This frame and the two sidings were taken out of use on 19th May, 1964. Today Colyton is the terminus of the Seaton Tramway and has a long loop with an intermediate crossover, the points being attractively placed in stone setts. There is a children's play area at the far end of the tramway.

Colyford

After leaving the station the gradient fell at 1 in 76/168 and crossed a lane by a girder bridge with 'Kerslake Exeter' cast on it. The length of about ¼ mile of 1 in 168 was curious in that for at least the last 20 years of the branch's existence, the gradient posts at both ends of this stretch pointed upwards! Colyford (2 m. 56 ch.) was simply a platform on the west side of the line and had no sidings or goods facilities. Accommodation varied over the years, but in its latter years shelter was offered by a pre-cast concrete hut.

Latterly a telephone was provided at Seaton adjacent to the former signal box and, immediately before a train's departure, the guard was required to advise the crossing keeper at Colyford that his train was about to leave. In the event of the guard not being able to contact the crossing keeper, the guard had to inform the driver to approach the crossing with caution and be prepared to find the gates closed across the line.

During the period when no member of staff was on duty at Colyford, down trains were brought to a stand at the home signal protecting the level crossing, whence the guard proceeded to the ground frame to place the gates across the road and lower the home signal to admit the train to the platform. After the train had cleared the crossing the signal was replaced to danger and the gates opened to the public. If the train was the last to pass over the branch for the day the guard also extinguished the platform lamps. Similar arrangements were in force for up trains. In all cases the guard was responsible for the collection of tickets. Light engines were prohibited from using the line when Colyford was unstaffed unless accompanied by a member of the traffic staff who opened and shut the gates.

At about 1.00 pm on 21st July, 1913, the 12.44 pm excursion train from Seaton Junction passed the home signal at danger and ran through the gates, which were closed across the line and demolished them. Driver H. Wilson was held responsible for the mishap and suffered suspension for one week.

When the porter arrived at the booking office on 27th June, 1929 he found that the outer door had been broken and the inside door forced open with the lock's screws wrenched off. The sum of £2 1s. 4d. was missing together with a suitcase, the property of Major Woodcock of Colyford.

Today the tramway has a passing loop at Colyford with two low platforms and a down bay, the latter not having an overhead electric wire. Before the level crossing a tram driver stops and uses a key to lower the barriers and obtain a white light to proceed.

Seaton

Between Colyford and Seaton the line followed the estuary of the Axe. Seaton station (4 m. 31 ch.), had an island platform. It was situated practically on the sea front adjoining Warner's Holiday Camp at the east end of the town and when war broke out in 1939, a special train brought detainees to this camp. The platforms were rather short and must have caused problems at peak periods. The eastern face was normally used, the other platform road kept for berthing stock. No engine release road was provided in the original layout and a train had to be backed out of the station to allow the engine to run round. The original signal box lay at the entrance to the yard.

On 22nd July, 1929 the SR's Traffic Officers' Conference considered and recommended the removal of the tablet instruments from the signal box to a new ground frame. The estimated cost of £572 for this alteration was expected to effect an annual staff saving of £307.

Ground frame 'A', adjacent to the stop blocks on Platform 1, came into use on 11th January, 1930, tablet instruments being transferred from the signal box, the latter only being used when No. 2 platform (the western one), was brought into operation. Ground frame 'B' replaced ground frame 'A' nearer the blocks of Platform 2 on 27th May, 1936. A new layout was introduced on 28th June, 1936 when both ground frame 'B' and the original signal box closed. A new brick-built box with 20 levers, 4 of which were spare was brought into use near the terminal end of the former No. 2 platform which now became No. 1; the old No. 1 being renumbered '2'. The crossover linking the two platform roads at the north end of the station was taken out of use on 27th May, 1936, allowing both platforms to be extended.

The timber-built engine shed, built by Messrs Birmingham for £200, was replaced by one of concrete blocks with a corrugated asbestos pitched roof and situated further south on the site of the cattle pens. As with the original shed, the coal stage and water tank were immediately outside the entrance. Doors were provided at the southern end of the shed, to enable the dock it was built against to be used for end-loading facilities. The new shed opened on 28th March, 1936. In 1926 the staff employed at the shed comprised five, including two pairs of drivers and firemen. Under the BR Southern Region, Seaton, a sub-shed of Exmouth Junction, was coded 72A and when Exmouth Junction came under Western Region jurisdiction, it was recoded 83D in December 1962, though not officially so designated until September 1963.

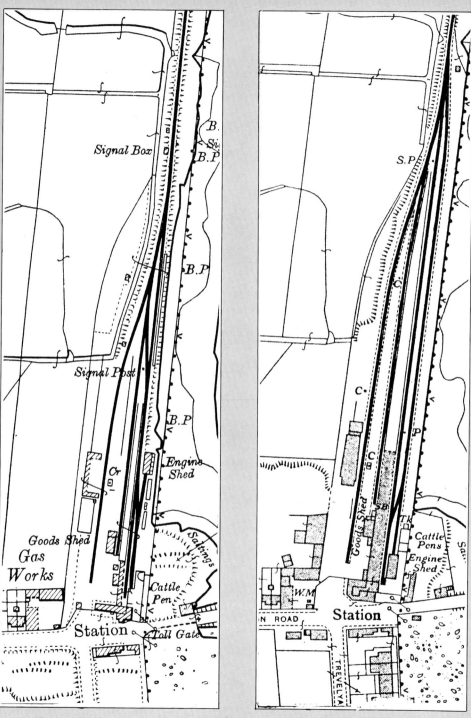

The branch terminus at Seaton showing (*left*) the 1905 Survey and (*right*) the 1936 plan. Note the position of the engine sheds.

Reproduced from the 25″, Ordnance Survey map

Ex-LBSCR 'D1' class 0–4–2T No. B214 seen here at Seaton c.1931 (allocated to the branch in June 1930). The coaches are the 1914 series 'gated' stock, probably Set 373. To the left of the locomotive's chimney is the water tank gauge. The pointer stands near the base of the [ ] [ ] [ ] rising at the bottom and indicating a full tank.

Lens of Sutton

SPECIAL EXCURSION

AUGUST BANK HOLIDAY
Monday, August 6th

TO

SEATON
AND
LYME REGIS

FROM	DEPART	RETURN FARES (Second Class) Seaton s. d.	Lyme Regis s. d.	Arrival on Return p.m.
TAUNTON	a.m. 11 0	6/3	6/3	9 15
THORNFALCON	11 15	5/9	6/3	9 5
HATCH	11 25	5/0	4/9	8 55
ILTON HALT	11 30	4/9	4/6	8 50
ILMINSTER	11 3	4/6	4/3	8 45
DONYATT HALT	11 45	4/3	4/3	8 40
CHARD CENTRAL	p.m. 12 20	4/3	4/0	8 30
CHARD JUNCTION		3/3	3/0	7 55

Seaton ... arr. p.m. 1 0
Lyme Regis ... 1 D

RETURN (same day) depart Seaton 7.15 p.m., Lyme Regis 7.10 p.m.

NOTE. ‡—Passengers for Lyme Regis change at Axminster in each direction.

Children under Three years of age, Free.
Three and under Fourteen years of age, half-fare (fractions of 1d. charged as 1d.).

Tickets can be obtained in advance at Booking Stations and Agencies.

No Worry, No Strain, Much Better by Train

Further information will be supplied on application to Booking Stations, Agencies, or to Mr. W. J. HARTNELL, District Superintendent, Exeter (St. David's) (Telephone Exeter 72281, Extension 301, 302, or 203); or to Mr. F. V. SPILLARD, District Manager, Exeter (Central) (Telephone Exeter 73181, Extension 25).

Paddington Station, W.2.
July, 1962.

E9—159   Bartlett & Son (Exeter) Ltd., 138 Cowick Street, Exeter

---

SOUTH WESTERN RAILWAY.

A DAY EXCURSION
TO
SEATON, SIDMOUTH,
AND
EXMOUTH
ON
EASTER MONDAY,
WILL RUN AS UNDER:—

	RETURN FARES.—Third Class. To Seaton or Sidmouth. s. d.	To Exmouth. s. d.
	7 6	8 6

		a.m.
Waterloo	dep.	6 30
Vauxhall	,,	6 35
Queen's Road	,,	6 13
Clapham Junction	,,	6 43
Chelsea	,,	6 10
West Brompton	,,	8 5
Kensington (Addison Road)	,,	8 52
Wimbledon	,,	6 52
Surbiton	,,	6 35
Hampton Court	,,	6 40
Thames Ditton	,,	7 26
Woking	,,	8 2
Basingstoke	,,	8 44
Seaton	arr.	10 44
Sidmouth	,,	11 54
Exmouth	,,	

The Return Train will leave Exmouth at 6.5 p.m., Sidmouth at 6.45 p.m., Seaton 7.30 p.m. on the same day only.

IN CONNECTION WITH THE ABOVE EXCURSION PASSENGERS WILL BE BOOKED FROM THE FOLLOWING STATIONS, AND BY THE TRAINS SHOWN:—

		a.m.			a.m.
Kingston	dep.		Brentford	dep.	8
Hampton Wick	,,		Kew Bridge	,,	8 12
Teddington	,,		Chiswick	,,	8 15
Strawberry Hill	,,		Barnes	,,	8 20
Twickenham	,,		Putney	,,	8 24
Richmond	,,		Windsor	,,	6 80
Mortlake	,,		Datchet	,,	6 34
Hounslow	,,		Wraysbury	,,	6 39
Isleworth	,,		Staines (High Street)	,,	6 45

Passengers change at Clapham Junction on the forward and return journey, except those from Windsor, Datchet, Wraysbury, and Staines, who change at Woking on the forward journey.
*Passengers alight at Staines Junction on the return.

CHAS. SCOTTER, General Manager.

Waterloo and Sons Limited, Printers, London Wall, London.

Handbills relating to the branch, the one on the left dated 1894, and the right, 1962.
Author's Collection

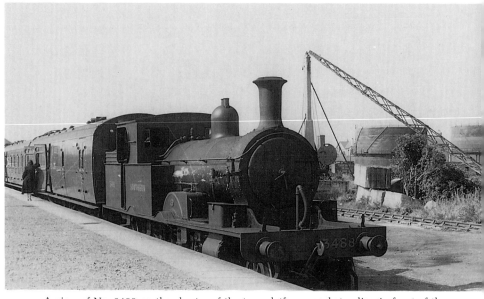

A view of No. 3488 on the shorter of the two platforms and standing in front of the stone yard on 9th July, 1949.   *H.C. Casserley*

The stop blocks end of platform No. 1 and the small signal box on the right, seen c.1960.   *Lens of Sutton*

The 'Odeon cinema' style architecture of the 1930s terminus is obvious in this c.1950 view. Day returns to Exeter are advertised for 4s. 9d. and car parking is 1 shilling!

Author's collection

'M7' class 0–4–4T No. 30046 stands at the coaling stage outside the locomotive shed, c.1960. Coach set No. 381 awaits its next journey at Platform No. 2.   *Lens of Sutton*

A view north during reconstruction of Seaton platform which is being widened and lengthened. The slewing of the platform line has entailed the removal of the line to the cattle pen (*right*); note the upturned loading gauge. 'S11' class 4–4–0 No. 399 is being watered on 1st June, 1936. *S.W. Baker*

A view from stop blocks. Note the concrete block-built engine shed (*right*) and the coaches in Platform No. 1 with the run round loop on the right in this 1960 view. *Lens of Sutton*

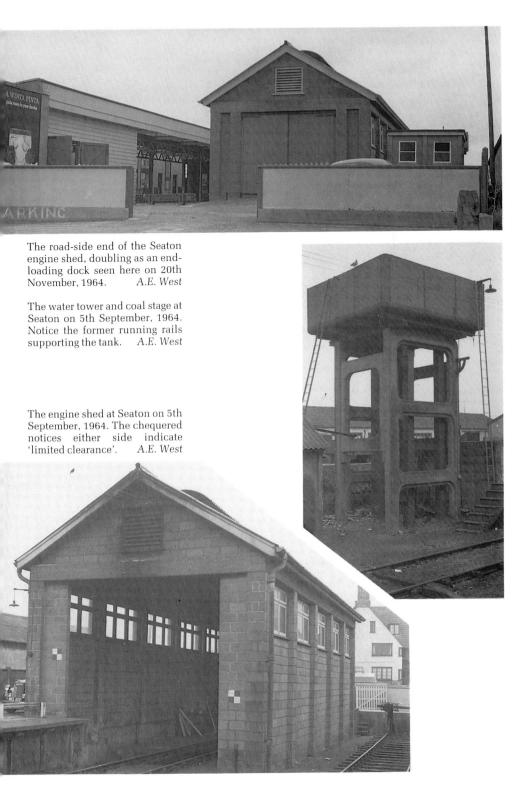

The road-side end of the Seaton engine shed, doubling as an end-loading dock seen here on 20th November, 1964.   A.E. West

The water tower and coal stage at Seaton on 5th September, 1964. Notice the former running rails supporting the tank.   A.E. West

The engine shed at Seaton on 5th September, 1964. The chequered notices either side indicate 'limited clearance'.   A.E. West

Two ex-GWR auto coaches at Platform No. 2 await the return of ex-GWR '64XX' class 0−6−0PT No. 6412 at present standing at the coaling stage. Note the platform canopy is glazed to give light; photographed on 26th October, 1963. *E. Wilmshurst*

A 'M7' class 0−4−4T No. 30048 fitted with air-controlled gear for motor-train operation, simmers at Seaton c.1960. *Lens of Sutton*

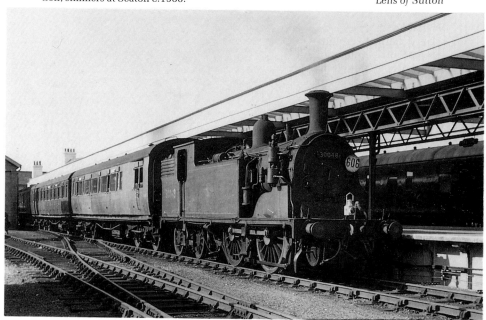

In 1936 the Italianate type station building was replaced by one in the SR concrete and brick style with a glass roof covering a greater length of platform. Even after modification the layout sometimes caused difficulties. One August Bank Holiday Monday three excursions were worked to Seaton. Two of the coach sets were stabled during the day at Seaton Junction, but one remained at Seaton, and to make room for it the goods yard had to be cleared, the empties being despatched and other wagons temporarily removed to Colyton. Some day excursion trains were run from as far afield as London.

A goods shed was provided and as part of the renewal programme it was given a cement rendering. At one time the yard dealt with a considerable stone traffic from the quarries at Beer but, unfortunately, the stone failed to live up to its early promise. Brilliant white and easy to carve, it proved unable to withstand the polluted sulphur-laden air of cities, which soiled it and caused the surface to break away. The large crane provided in the yard progressively had less and less work and was removed when the station was remodelled.

The gas works immediately west of the station brought coal traffic to the branch and although plans for a private siding to the premises were agreed in 1909, these never came to fruition.

As it was an 'open' station, a ticket platform was sited outside Seaton and working timetables carried a note that 'All Down passenger trains must stop at the ticket platform during the months June–September for the collection of tickets.' The 1888 Ordnance Survey map showed the ticket platform as an island at the north end of the layout, but on the 1903 edition it appeared east of the line.

The severe winter of 1963 froze the water column at Seaton. As the timetable did not permit a locomotive to run to Axminster where the nearest supply could be obtained, Exmouth Junction shed sent a Pacific to work services until the branch 'M7' was refilled by hose pipe from Seaton station toilet. After an hour it had sufficient water to reach Axminster, but the Pacific remained for two days working some of the trains.

With the advent of dieselisation, Seaton locomotive depot was closed on 4th November, 1963, the signal box suffering the same fate on 2nd May, 1965, when, apart from the line serving Platform No. 2, all track was taken out of use. Racal Seaton Limited's works are now on the site of the passenger station.

London and South Western Ry.

787

TO

SEATON

ON AND AFTER 16th MARCH,

And until Further Notice.

COLYTON AND SEATON BRANCH.

This is a Single Line, and only one engine is allowed to be upon it at one time.

Distance from Colyton Junction.	DOWN TRAINS.—WEEK DAYS.						No Sunday Trains.
	STATIONS.	1 Pas.	2 Pas. & Gds	3 Pas.	4 Pas.	5 Pas.	
Miles.		a.m. 1 2 3	a.m. 1 2 3	p.m. 1 2 3	p.m. 1 2	p.m. 1 2	
	Axminster ....dep.	...	...	...	3 5	...	
	Colyton Junction... arr.	...	...	...	3 13	...	
	Do. do. ...dep.	8 50	11 15	12 40	3 18	5 30	
	Colyton Town ...... ,,	8 57	11 30	12 48	3 26	5 38	
2¾	Colyford .... ,,	9 1	11 35	12 52	3 30	5 42	
4¼	Seaton .... arr.	9 8	11 45	12 58	3 36	5 48	

Distance from Seaton.	UP TRAINS.—WEEK DAYS.						No Sunday Trains.
	STATIONS.	1 Pas.	2 Pas.	3 Gds. & Pas.	4 Pas. & Gds.	5 Pas.	
Miles.		a.m. 1 2 3	a.m. 1 2	noon 1 2 3	p.m. 1 2	p.m. 1 2	
1½	Seaton ....dep.	8 0	10 35	12 0	1 30	4 20	
2½	Colyford .... ,,	8 7	10 42	12 6	1 37	4 27	
4½	Colyton Town .... ,,	8 11	10 46	12 10	1 41	4 31	
	Colyton Junction ....arr.	8 19	10 54	12 21	1 49	4 39	
	do, do. ....dep.	...	...	...	1 54	...	
	Axminster ....arr.	...	...	...	2 2	...	

The March 1868 Working Timetable for the branch. By the July of 1868, two more trains were added in the evening service.

A further c.1910 view of Colyton station showing the station buildings and signal box with the village in the background.   *J.J. Hurd Collection*

Chapter Three
Timetables and Traffic

The line opened with a service of four down passenger trains, plus one mixed train, with three passenger and two mixed trains in the reverse direction. No trains were run on Sundays. Passenger trains were scheduled to take 18 minutes on the down journey and 19 minutes on the up. The down mixed train took 30 minutes and the up mixed trains 24 and 19 minutes. The branch engine worked the mixed train through from Seaton to Axminster and returned with a through passenger train.

In May 1868 the service was increased to four down passenger trains plus two mixed and five up passenger trains plus one mixed, while the following month the service was further increased by an extra passenger train each way. In November the timetable reverted to that run in May.

August 1874 saw seven passenger trains each way taking about 17 minutes, one through train running to and from Axminster. In addition a mixed train ran in each direction along the branch. In August 1887 there were nine down and ten up trains with one through working to and from Axminster, passenger trains taking 15 minutes. In the winter timetable for 1st October, 1903 to 31st May, 1904, seven down and eight up passenger trains ran on weekdays. Additionally two mixed and one goods train ran in the down direction and one mixed, one goods and one conditional goods in the opposite direction. A Colyton–London vacuum market wagon was sent by the 1.20 pm passenger train ex-Seaton.

From 1st June to 30th September, 1909, nine passenger trains ran each way plus two mixed trains in each direction, one goods and a conditional goods. From 7th July to 15th September a through Great Western excursion via Chard ran on Wednesdays. In the timetable for the period 7th June to 30th September, 1914, nine passenger trains ran each way taking mostly 14 minutes, though one down train which omitted the stop at Colyford made the journey in 12 minutes. One down goods ran and in the up direction, one mixed train and one goods.

In the summer of 1938, 13 passenger trains were scheduled each way on Mondays to Fridays, with an additional return working on Thursdays. One of the trains ran through to Axminster. The freight train was the first working of the day and left Seaton at 6.00 am, returning at 7.30 am. Journey times for passenger trains varied between 12 and 16 minutes and the 1.12 pm down was permitted to run mixed if required. On Saturdays the service increased to 14 down and 15 up passenger trains, plus the freight. No train was mixed, but the Axminster through service operated. An additional locomotive came from Exmouth Junction to work three down and four up services. Thirteen down and 14 up trains were provided on Sundays, with several worked by an engine sent specially from Exeter.

The 1938 summer timetable showed through coaches on the 11.00 am ex-Waterloo being sent forward from Salisbury on Mondays–Fridays by the 12.38 pm slow, and in the reverse direction being attached to the 9.00 am Ilfracombe–Salisbury slow for forwarding on the 12.30 pm from Exeter. On

SEATON BRANCH.—WEEK DAYS—NO SUNDAY SERVICE.

An extract from the Summer 1909 Working Timetable for the Branch.

FOR SPEED RESTRICTIONS SEE PAGES A, B, C & D.

This is a Single Line and is worked under the Regulations for working Single Lines by the Electric Train Tablet Block System.

All Down Passenger Trains will stop at the Ticket platform at Seaton during June, July, August and September in each year for the Collection of Tickets.

DOWN TRAINS.

	1 Goods when required	2 Goods and Passenger	3 Goods B	4 Passenger	5 Passenger	6 Passenger	7 Passenger	8 Pass.	9 Goods and Passenger	10 Passenger	11 Passenger	12 Passenger	13 Passenger	14 Passenger	15 Exp. Cars and Goods Thurs & Sat Aug only
Seaton Jc.															
Colyton															
Colyford															
Seaton															

UP TRAINS.

	1 Goods when required	2 Goods & Passenger	3 Goods	4 Passenger	5 Pass.	6 Passenger	7 Passenger	8 Pass.	9 Passenger	10 Passenger	11 Passenger	12 Passenger	13 Passenger	14 Passenger	15 Passenger Thurs & Sat July & Aug only
Seaton															
Colyford															
Colyton															
Seaton J.															

A Colyton and Seaton Junction to advise Seaton when this Train is required to run. Seaton to arrange and advise all concerned.
B West No. 4 Down run No. 3 Down will start at 9.5 a.m. and run 5 minutes earlier throughout.

SEATON BRANCH.—WEEK DAYS—NO SUNDAY SERVICE.— The Working Timetable for September 1914.

This is a Single Line and is worked under the Regulations for working Single Lines by the Electric Train Tablet Block System.

All Down Passenger Trains will stop at the Ticket platform at Seaton during June, July, August and September in each year for the Collection of Tickets.

For Special Instructions as to the load of Trains on this Branch during certain portions of the year, see page 76 of the Appendix to the Book of Rules and Regulations and Working Time Tables, dated 1st January, 1911.

DOWN TRAINS.

	1 Passenger	2 Passenger	3 Goods	4 Passenger	5 Passenger	6 Passenger	7 Passenger	8 Pass.	9 Passenger	10 Passenger	11 Passenger	12 Passenger	13 Passenger	14 Passenger	15 Passenger	16 Exp. Cars and Goods Thurs July & Aug only
Seaton Jc.																
Colyton																
Colyford																
Seaton																

UP TRAINS.

	1 Passenger	2 Passenger	3 Goods	4 Passenger	5 Passenger	6 Pass.	7 Passenger	8 Passenger	9 Passenger	10 Passenger	11 Passenger	12 Goods & Passenger	13 Passenger	14 Passenger	15 Passenger & Aug only
Seaton															
Colyford															
Colyton															
Seaton J.															

Saturdays there were coaches on the 9.01 am, 12.09 pm and 3.24 pm from Waterloo and in the up direction the 9.55 am, 11.30 am from Exeter and the 2.12 pm Seaton–London. These Monday–Friday arrangements continued through the winter on all weekdays.

The 1938/9 winter service consisted of 13 passenger trains and one freight each way on weekdays, the mixed and Axminster workings continuing. A Sunday service of nine down and ten up trains was scheduled to commence on 7th May, 1939. The timetable for 2nd July to 24th September, 1939 showed 13 trains each way daily with an additional one on Saturday, when one down train omitted the Colyford stop and two up trains ran non-stop, taking 8 and 10 minutes; 13 Sunday trains ran in each direction.

In October 1947, 13 passenger trains ran in each direction on weekdays and four on Sundays. The Monday–Friday timetable for the summer of 1948 showed 13 passenger trains each way rising to 15 on Saturdays. Six return workings were made on Sundays increasing to seven in 1949. In the following years slight variations were made – in 1950 12 trains ran Mondays –Fridays and 16 on Saturdays and 13 and 17 respectively in 1951. The Axminster through train and one working each way mixed when required still continued to appear. The Sunday service rose to eight in 1951 and nine in 1953. A winter service of four trains each way was shown in the 1951–2 timetable, but by 1953–4 only ran from Easter. The year 1959 brought a peak of 15 passenger trains each way on Mondays–Fridays, 18 on Saturdays and 10 on Sundays.

In 1948 through coaches ran on the 10.50 am (later 11.00) from Waterloo, and the 9.35 am Exeter, the latter taking them to Templecombe for attachment to the following 10.30 am. In the down direction the arrangements were as pre-war. The service was increased on summer Saturdays with coaches on the 11.47 am (10.35 from 1949; 10.45 from 1953) from Waterloo, supplemented by the 7.50 am (later 8.05) from 1950 and the 8.22 am as well from 1954. In the opposite direction there were coaches on the 8.30 am Exeter, joined by the 9.08 am Exmouth in 1950 (these were transferred to the 10.00 Exeter, later 9.45 Budleigh Salterton, then 9.38 Littleham by 1953) and 2.35 pm Seaton (1.45 pm Exmouth from 1955) in 1953.

The period 1950/1 showed a working for a '415' 4–4–2 tank engine which ran as follows: 6.55 am light engine Exmouth Junction–Axminster; pilot 8.32 am to Lyme Regis; 9.00 am to Axminster with the Waterloo coaches; 11.35 am to Lyme with through coaches from Waterloo; 12.10 pm to Axminster, then 1.28 pm light engine to Seaton Junction where it worked the 2.20 pm to Seaton; assisted the 2.40 pm to Seaton Junction and 3.56 pm to Exeter Central (12.56 pm from Salisbury). Meanwhile an 'M7' ran at 6.15 am light engine from Exmouth Junction to Seaton; assisted the 9.00 am to Seaton Junction (Waterloo coaches); ran light engine 9.15 am to Seaton; worked the 10.10 am to Seaton Junction (Waterloo coaches) and ran 11.00 am light engine to Exmouth Junction.

On weekdays in 1958 a through coach ran to Waterloo. It was attached to the 8.25 am from Seaton and then was worked back alone, the branch set being left at the junction. This was in order to allow the through coach to be

SEATON BRANCH.

Summer Service, July 3rd to September 23rd.

MONDAYS TO FRIDAYS, JULY 3rd TO SEPTEMBER 22nd ONLY.

To Seaton.

	Distances.			—	1m. 49c.	2m. 41c.	4m. 16c.
				Seaton Junc. dep.	Colyton. dep.	Coly-ford. dep.	Seaton. arr.
a.m.	*Engine* ...	Th.O.	...	*6‖35*	...	*6‡42* *6 45*	*6‖49*
,,	Freight ...	...	...	7 30	7‡36 7 50	7‡54 7 58	8 4
,,	Pass ...	...	...	8 43	8 47½	8 50½	8 55
,,	,, ...	...	...	9 36	9 40½	9 43½	9 48
,,	,, ...	...	...	10 40	10 44½	10 47½	10 52
p.m.	Pass ...	...	...	12 36	12 40½	12 43½	12 48
,,	,, ...	...	...	1 12	1 16½	1 19½ 1 22½	1 27
,,	,, ...	...	G	1 58	2 2½	2 5½	2 10
,,	*Mixed* ...	...	Q	*1 58*	*2‡ 3* *2 8½*	*2‡11½* *2 14½*	*2 19*
,,	Pass ...	...	...	2 50	2 54½	2 57½	3 2
,,	,, ...	...	...	4 33	4 37½	4 40½	4 45
,,	,, ...	...	...	5 36	5 40½	5 43½	5 48
,,	,, ...	...	...	6 36	6 40½	6‡43 6 46	6 51
,,	,, ...	...	...	7 50	7 54½	7‡57 8 0	8 5
,,	,, ...	...	...	8 44	8 48½	8‡51 8 54	8 59
,,	,, ...	...	E	9 43	9 47½	9‡50 9 53	0 50
,,	,, ...	Th.O.	...	*10 21*	*10 25½*	*10‡28* *10 31*	*1036*

From Seaton.

	Distances.			—	1m. 31c.	2m. 47c.	4m. 16c.
				Seaton. dep.	Coly-ford. dep.	Colyton. dep.	Seaton Junc. arr.
a.m.	*Freight* ...	Th.O.	...	*5 30*	*5‡36* *5 40*	*5‡44* *6 4*	*6 10*
,,	*Pass.* ...	Th.O.	...	*6 55*	*7‡ 0* *7 3*	*7 7*	*7 11*
,,	Freight ...	Th.X	...	6 0	6‡ 6 6 10	6‡14 6 34	6 40
,,	Pass. ...	...	...	8 22	8 27	8 31	8 35
,,	,, ...	...	...	9 10	9 15	9 19	9 23
,,	,, ...	...	...	10 15	10 20	10 24	10 28
,,	,, ...	...	C	11 48	11 53	11 57	12 1
p.m.	,, ...	...	...	12 53	12 58	1 2	1 6
,,	,, ...	...	...	1 35	1‡40 1 42	1 46	1 50
,,	,, ...	...	...	2 27	2 32	2 36	2 40
,,	,, ...	...	...	3 55	4 0	4 4	4 8
,,	,, ...	...	...	4 50	4 55	4‡59 5 2	5 6
,,	,, ...	...	...	6 10	6‡15 6 18	6 22	6 26
,,	,, ...	...	...	7 30	7‡35 7 38	7 42	7 46
,,	,, ...		...	8 15	8‡20 8 23	8 27	8 31
,,	,, ...	...	D	9 4	9‡ 9 9 12	9 16	9 20
,,	,, ...	Th.O.	...	*10 3*	*10‡8* *1011*	*10 15*	*10 19*

SATURDAYS, JULY 8th TO SEPTEMBER 23rd ONLY.

To Seaton.

				Seaton Junc. dep.	Colyton. dep.	Coly-ford. dep.	Seaton. arr.
a.m.	Freight ...	...	...	7 30	7‡36 7 50	7‡54 7 58	8 4
,,	Pass ...	...	...	8 43	8 47½	8 50½	8 55
,,	,, ...	...	...	9 36	9 40½	9 43½	9 48
,,	,, ...	...	A	10 53	10 57½	11 0½	11 5
,,	,, ...	...	...	11 33	11 37½	11 40½	11 45
p.m.	*Engine* ...	...	Q	*12‖30*	...	...	*12‖40*
,,	Pass ...	...	AB	12 52	12 56½	...	1 4
,,	,, ...	...	...	1 34	1 38½	1 41½	1 46
,,	,, ...	...	...	2 35	2 39½	2 40½	2 47
,,	,, ...	...	AB	3 20	3 24½	3 27½	3 32
,,	,, ...	...	...	4 38	4 42½	4 45½	4 50
,,	,, ...	...	...	5 36	5 40½	5 43½	5 48
,,	,, ...	...	BF	7 8	7 12½	7‡15 7 18	7 23
,,	,, ...	...	...	8 1	8 5½	8‡ 8 8 11	8 16
,,	,, ...	...	...	8 44	8 48½	8‡51 8 54	8 59
,,	,, ...	...	E	9 43	9 47½	9‡50 9 53	9 58

From Seaton.

				Seaton. dep.	Coly-ford. dep.	Colyton. dep.	Seaton Junc. arr.
a.m.	Freight ...	...	...	6 0	6‡ 6 6 10	6‡14 6 34	6 40
,,	Pass. ...	...	...	8 22	8 27	8 31	8 35
,,	,, ...	...	...	9 10	9 15	9 19	9 23
,,	,, ...	...	...	10 2	10 7	10 11	10 15
,,	,, ...	...	AC	10 23	10 28	10 32	10 36
,,	,, ...	...	AC	11 52	11 57	12 1	12 5
p.m.	,, ...	...	...	12 15	...	...	12 23
,,	*Scouts* ...	...	Q	*1 10*	...	...	*1 20*
,,	Pass. ...	...	...	1 50	1 55	1 59	2 3
,,	,, ...	...	AC	2 20	...	...	2 30
,,	,, ...	...	...	2 55	3 0	3 4	3 8
,,	,, ...	...	A	3 42	3 47	3 51	3 55
,,	,, ...	...	...	5 5	5 10	5‡13 5 17	5 21
,,	,, ...	...	...	6 10	6‡15 6 18	6 22	6 26
,,	,, ...	...	...	7 40	7‡45 7 48	7 52	7 56
,,	,, ...	...	...	8 20	8‡25 8 28	8 32	8 36
,,	,, ...	...	D	9 4	9† 9 9 12	9 16	9 20

A—Exeter engine.
B—Through coach from Waterloo.
C—Through coach for Waterloo.
D—To Axminster.
E—From Axminster.
F—Run 5 minutes later when 3.24 p.m.Q Waterloo runs.
G—Will not apply when 1.58 p.m. Q Mixed runs.
‡—Arrive.

SUNDAYS—JULY 2nd TO SEPTEMBER 24th only.

		Timing No.		Seaton J. dep.	Colyton. dep.	Colyfr'd. dep.	Seaton. arr.
a.m.	*Engine*	...	Q	*9‖35*	...	...	*9‖50*
,,	Pass.	...	...	10 28	10 32½	10 35½	10 40
,,	Pass.	...	...	11 24	11 28½	11 31½	11 36
p.m	Pass.	...	E	12 16	12 20½	12 23½	12 28
,,	N.S.L.	239/287	CD	12 35	12 39½	12 42½	12 47
,,	*Excn.*	*285*	A	*1 20*	...	...	*1 30*
,,	Pass.	...	...	1 54	1 58½	2 1½	2 6
,,	Pass.	...	...	2 50	2 54½	2 57½	3 2
,,	Pass.	...	...	3 45	3 49½	3 52½	3 57
,,	Pass.	...	...	4 35	4 39½	4 42½	4 47
,,	Pass.	...	...	5 55	5 59½	6 2½	6 7
,,	Engine	...	E	6‖55	...	...	7‖ 5
,,	Pass.	...	...	7 30	7 34½	7 37½	7 42
,,	Pass.	...	...	8 10	8 14½	8‡17 8 20	8 25
,,	Pass.	...	B	9 5	9 9½	9‡12 9 15	9 20
,,	Excn.	307/296/ 309	F	10 30	10 34½	10‡38 10 40	10 45

		Timing No.		Seaton. dep.	Colyf'rd. dep.	Colyton. dep.	Seaton J. arr.
a.m.	*Empty*	...	Q	*9 0*	...	...	*9 15*
,,	Pass.	...	...	10 0	10 5	10 9	10 13
,,	Pass.	...	...	11 5	11 10	11 14	11 18
,,	Pass.	...	...	11 45	11 50	11 54	11 58
p.m.	Engine	...	EG	12‖50	...	...	1‖ 0
,,	*Empty*	*285*	A	*1† 5*	...	...	*1†15*
,,	Pass.	...	...	1 35	1 40	1 44	1 48
,,	Pass.	...	...	2 15	2 20	2 24	2 28
,,	Pass.	...	...	3 15	3 20	3 24	3 28
,,	Pass.	...	...	4 15	4 20	4 24	4 28
,,	Pass.	...	...	5 30	5 35	5 39	5 43
,,	Pass.	...	...	6 40	6 45	6 49	6 53
,,	N.S.L.	239	EF	7 12	7 17	7 22	7 26
,,	Pass.	...	...	7 48	7‡53 7 56	8 0	8 4
,,	Pass.	...	...	8 31	8‡36 8 39	8 43	8 47
,,	Excn.	307/309	F	9 45	9‡50 9 53	9 57	10 1

A—Runs July 16th, Aug. 27th only.
B—Convey empty stock for Seaton if required.
C—On Aug. 6th only run as Company's excursion.
D—On July 9th, 16th, Aug. 13th, 27th, and Sept. 10th only, run 10 minutes later.
E—Exeter Engine.
F—Available for ordinary passengers.
G—Depart Seaton 12.33 p.m. arrive Seaton Jct. 12.43 p.m. on July 9th, 16th, Aug. 13th, 27th, and Sept. 10th.
‡—Arrive.

The summer and winter Working Timetables of 1939 for the branch.

SEATON BRANCH.

Winter Service, commencing September 25th—Weekdays only.

a.m.	Engine	Th. O.	Seaton Junc. dep.	Colyton. dep.	Coly-ford. dep.	Seaton. arr.
a.m.	Engine	Th. O.	6‖35	—	{6‡42 / 6 45}	6‖49
"	Freight	... ...	7 30	{7‡36 / 7 50}	{7‡54 / 7 58}	8 4
"	Pass.	... ...	8 43	8 47½	8 50½	8 55
"	Pass.	... ...	9 36	9 40½	9 43½	9 48
"	Pass.	... ...	10 40	10 44½	10 47½	10 52
p.m.	Pass.	... ...	12 36	12 40½	12 43½	12 48
"	Pass.	... ...	1 12	1 16½	{119½ / 122½}	1 27
"	Pass.	C	1 58	2 2½	2 5½	2 10
"	Mixed	Q	1 58	{2‡ 3 / 2 8½}	{211½ / 214½}	2 19
"	Pass.	A	2 50	2 54½	2 57½	3 2
"	Pass.	...	4 33	4 37½	4 40½	4 45
"	Pass.	...	5 36	5 40½	5 43½	5 48
"	Pass.	...	6 36	6 40½	{6‡43 / 6 46}	6 51
"	Pass.	...	7 50	7 54½	{7‡57 / 8 0}	8 5
"	Pass.	...	8 44	8 48½	{8‡51 / 8 54}	8 59
"	Pass.	B	9 43	9 47½	{9‡50 / 9 53}	9 58

			Seaton. dep.	Coly-ford. dep.	Coly-ton. dep.	Seaton Junc. arr.
a.m.	Freight	Th. O. ...	5 30	{5‡36 / 3 40}	{5‡44 / 6 4}	6 10
"	Pass.	Th. O. ...	6 55	{7‡ 0 / 7 3}	7 7	7 11
"	Freight	Th. X. ...	6 0	{6‡ 6 / 6 10}	{6‡14 / 6 34}	6 40
"	Pass.	... ...	8 22	8 27	8 31	8 35
"	Pass.	... ...	9 10	9 15	9 19	9 23
"	Pass.	... ...	10 15	10 20	10 24	10 28
"	Pass.	D	11 50	11 55	11 59	12 3
p.m.	Pass.	... ...	12 53	12 58	1 2	1 6
"	Pass.	... ...	1 35	{1‡40 / 1 42}	1 46	1 50
"	Pass.	... ...	2 27	2 32	2 36	2 40
"	Pass.	... ...	3 55	4 0	4 4	4 8
"	Pass.	... ...	4 50	4 55	{4‡59 / 5 2}	5 6
"	Pass.	... ...	6 10	{6‡15 / 6 18}	6 22	6 26
"	Pass.	... ...	7 30	{7‡35 / 7 33}	7 42	7 46
"	Pass.	... ...	8 15	{8‡20 / 8 23}	8 27	8 31
"	Pass.	E	9 4	{9‡ 9 / 9 12}	9 16	9 20

A—Conveys through coach from Waterloo.   Run 11 minutes later Saturdays only commencing June 1st, 1940.
B—From Axminster.
C—Will not apply when 1.58 Q Mixed runs.
D—Conveys through coach for Waterloo.
E—To Axminster.
‡—Arrive.

SUNDAYS, commencing May 5th, 1940.

			Seaton Junc. dep.	Colyton. dep.	Coly-ford. dep.	Seaton. arr.
a.m.	Pass.	... ...	10 28	10 32½	10 35½	10 40
"	Pass.	... ...	11 24	11 28½	11 31½	11 36
p.m.	Pass. and N.S.L.	...	12 35	12 39½	12 42½	12 47
"	Pass.	... ...	2 58	3 2½	3 5½	3 10
"	Pass.	... ...	4 25	4 29½	4 32½	4 37
"	Pass.	... ...	5 43	5 47½	5 50½	5 55
"	Pass.	... ...	7 32	7 36½	7 39½	7 44
"	Pass.	... ...	8 12	8 16½	{8‡19 / 8 22}	8 27
"	Pass.	... ...	9 5	9 9½	{9‡12 / 9 15}	9 20

			Seaton. dep.	Coly-ford. dep.	Coly-ton. dep.	Seaton Junc. arr.
a.m.	Pass.	... ...	10 0	10 5	10 9	10 13
"	Pass.	... ...	11 5	11 10	11 14	11 18
"	Pass.	... ...	11 45	11 50	11 54	11 58
p.m.	Pass.	... ...	2 17	2 22	2 26	2 30
"	Pass.	... ...	3 32	3 37	3 41	3 45
"	Pass.	... ...	5 15	5 20	5 24	5 28
"	Pass.	... ...	6 55	7 0	7 4	7 8
"	Return N.S.L.	...	7 12	7 17	7 22	7 26
"	Pass.	... ...	7 52	7 57	8 1	8 5
"	Pass.	... ...	8 42	{8‡47 / 8 50}	8 54	8 58

‡—Arrive.

thoroughly warmed before passengers joined it at Seaton. From Seaton Junction it was worked to Templecombe by the 9.35 am stopping train from Exeter Central to Templecombe, where it was attached to the 10.30 am Exeter Central to Waterloo. Similarly a down through coach was detached at Templecombe from the 1.00 pm ex-Waterloo and arrived at Seaton 4.57 pm.

On summer Saturdays much greater accommodation had to be provided for holidaymakers, the 1959 pattern being:

Up
9.00 am Seaton, two through coaches attached to 8.30 am Exeter Central.
10.20 am Seaton, six coaches attached to 9.38 am Littleham.
2.35 pm Seaton, six coaches attached to 1.45 pm Exmouth.

Down
8.05 am Waterloo–Exmouth, two coaches for Seaton, arrive 11.37 am.
8.22 am Waterloo–Ilfracombe, four coaches for Seaton, arrive 11.50 am.
10.45 am Waterloo–Seaton, five coaches, arrive 2.05 pm.

The formation of the 10.45 am from Waterloo included a buffet car which was required to return on the 2.35 pm Seaton to Waterloo. As only 30 minutes lay-over time was allowed at Seaton, on occasions when the down train was late, the buffet car was detached at Seaton Junction in order that it could be coupled to the up train.

On summer Saturdays in the latter days of steam working, the 12.05 pm ex-Seaton push-pull set was piloted in order to work an engine back to Seaton Junction following the consecutive arrival of two trains from Waterloo.

From the winter of 1961–2 there were no trains on Sundays outside the summer service, buses to and from Axminster being shown instead. From 9th September, 1963, trains were second class only. In summer 1964 the service was reduced to 11 trains on Mondays–Fridays, 14 on Saturdays and 10 on Sundays. Some improvement took place in the summer of 1965 with 13, 16 and 8 trains respectively. After dieselisation the last train up the branch was attached at Seaton Junction to the multiple unit which had been working on the Lyme Regis branch and was advertised as a through train to Exeter. In the morning it came up empty.

In 1962, the last year of the Monday to Friday through coaches, these came down on the 1.00 pm Waterloo, and were transferred to the 3.34 pm stopping train at Templecombe. In the up direction, the Saturday 8.30 am Exeter was replaced by a 9.30 am Exmouth with through Seaton coaches. All through coaches stopped in 1963.

Excursions were worked through from the GWR or Western Region stations such as Taunton and Ilminster, an SR engine replacing the Western locomotive at Chard Junction. In order to make room for berthing excursion coaches, wagons had to be temporarily transferred from Seaton to Colyton and if more than one excursion arrived, the coaches were stored at Seaton Junction.

On Whit Monday 1900, 835 passengers booked from Chard, while the same day in 1909 saw 5,000 trippers arrive by rail, including 526 from London.

70

SEATON BRANCH.

WEEKDAYS — Will not apply on SATURDAYS, 23rd JUNE to 22nd SEPTEMBER, 1951.

m. c.	DOWN	• a.m.	• a.m.	• a.m.	• a.m.	• p.m.	• p.m.	A • p.m.		Q Mixed. p.m.	G • p.m.	• p.m.		• p.m.	• p.m.	• p.m.	9.33 p.m. Axminster • p.m.
0 0	Seaton Jct. (T)	8 5	8 45	9 40	10 45	12 2	12 43	1 53	.	*1 53*	3 15	4 48	.	5 36	6 54	8 44	9 42
1 49	Colyton arr.	...	..	...	...	...	...	...	...	*1 58*	...	...	...	...	...	...	...
	Colyton dep.	8 9½	8 49½	9 44½	10 49½	12 6½	12 47½	1 57½	.	*2 3½*	3 19½	4 52½	.	5 40½	6 58½	8 48½	9 46½
2 41	Colyford arr.	...	...	...	...	...	12 50½	2 0½	...	*2 6½*	...	4 55	...	5 43	7 1	8 51	9 49
	Colyford dep.	8 12½	8 52½	9 47½	10 52½	12 9½	12 53½	2 3½	.	*2 9½*	3 22½	4 58	.	5 46	7 4	8 54	9 52
4 16	Seaton ... (T)	8 17	8 57	9 52	10 57	12 14	12 58	2 8	...	*2 14*	3 27	5 3	...	5 51	7 9	8 59	9 57

m. c.	UP	• a.m.	• a.m.	• a.m.	H • a.m.	• a.m.	• p.m.	• p.m.	Commences 24th September.	• p.m.	Until 21st September.	• p.m.	E • p.m.	• p.m.	• p.m.	• p.m.	To Axminster. • p.m.
0 0	Seaton ...	7 46	8 23	9 10	10 3	11 44	12 22	1 28		2 35		2 45	3 48	5 8	6 10	8 15	9 3
1 31	Colyford arr.	...	...	...	...	...	...	1 33		...		...	...	5 13	6 15	8 20	9 8
	Colyford dep.	7 51	8 28	9 15	10 8	11 49	12 27	1 35		2 40		2 50	3 53	5 16	6 18	8 23	9 11
2 47	Colyton arr.	...	...	...	...	...	...	...		..		...	3 57	...	...	...	...
	Colyton dep.	7 55	8 32	9 19	10 12	11 53	12 31	1 39		2 44		2 54	4 2	5 20	6 22	8 27	9 15
4 16	Seaton Jct. ...	7 59	8 36	9 23	10 16	11 57	12 35	1 43		2 48		2 58	4 6	5 24	6 26	8 31	9 19

SATURDAYS ONLY, 23rd JUNE to 22nd SEPTEMBER, 1951.

DOWN	6‖15 a.m. Engine Exm'hJc FM a.m.	• a.m.	• a.m.	Engine FD a.m.	• a.m.	• a.m.	C • a.m.	• p.m.	• p.m.	10.35 a.m. W'loo. p.m.	• p.m.	• p.m.	• p.m.	• p.m.	• p.m.	• p.m.	• p.m.	• p.m.	9.33 p.m. Axminster • p.m.
Seaton Jct. (T)	7‖30	8 5	8 40	9‖15	9 40	10 35	11 25	12 35	1 10	1 55	2 20	3 10	4 0	4 48	5 36	6 55	7 55	8 44	9 42
Colyton arr.	...	...	...	...	...	...	...	...	...	...	...	...	...	...	...	...	...	...	...
Colyton dep.	.	8 9½	8 44½	.	9 44½	10 39½	11 29½	12 39½	1 14½	.	2 24½	3 14½	4 4½	4 52½	5 40½	6 59½	7 59½	8 48½	9 46½
Colyford arr.	...	...	...	...	...	...	...	...	...	...	...	...	...	4 55	5 43	7 2	8 2	8 51	9 49
Colyford dep.	.	8 12½	8 47½	.	9 47½	10 42½	11 32½	12 42½	1 17½	.	2 27½	3 17½	4 7½	4 58	5 46	7 5	8 5	8 54	9 52
Seaton (T)	7‖M40	8 17	8 52	9‖D25	9 52	10 47	11 37	12 47	1 22	2 5	2 32	3 22	4 12	5 3	5 51	7 10	8 10	8 59	9 57

UP	• a.m.	• a.m.	To W'loo. • a.m.	• a.m.	FH a.m.	• a.m.	• p.m.	• p.m.	• p.m.	• p.m.	• p.m.	• p.m.	• p.m.	• p.m.	• p.m.	• p.m.	To Axminster • p.m.
Seaton ...	7 46	8 23	9 0	9 55	10 10	10 58	12 8	12 55	1 26	2 40	3 40	4 20	5 8	6 10	7 35	8 15	9 3
Colyford arr.	...	...	...	...	...	...	...	...	...	...	...	...	5 13	6 15	7 40	8 20	9 8
Colyford dep.	7 51	8 28	.	10 0	.	11 3	12 13	12 58	1 31	2 45	3 45	4 25	5 16	6 18	7 43	8 23	9 11
Colyton arr.	...	...	...	...	...	...	...	...	...	...	...	4 29	...	...	...	...	...
Colyton dep.	7 55	8 32	9 7	10 4	.	11 7	12 17	1 4	1 35	2 49	3 49	4 32	5 20	6 22	7 47	8 27	9 15
Seaton Jct. ...	7 59	8 36	9 11	10 8	10 21	11 11	12 21	1 8	1 39	2 53	3 53	4 36	5 24	6 26	7 51	8 31	9 19

SUNDAYS, 24th JUNE TO 23rd SEPTEMBER, 1951, INCLUSIVE.

DOWN	• a.m.		• p.m.		• N Excn. No.207 p.m.	• p.m.	• p.m.			• p.m.			J • p.m.		• p.m.		Excn. No.263 • L. p.m.
Seaton Jct.	11 17	.	12 5	.	*12 40*	2 28	3 5	.	.	4 20	.	.	7 25	.	8 15	.	10 15
Colyton ...	11 21½	...	12 9½	...	...	2 32½	3 9½	...	...	4 24½	...	...	7 29½	...	8 19½	...	10 19½
Colyford arr.	.	.	.	.	.	.	.	.	.	.	.	.	.	.	8 22	.	10 22
Colyford dep.	11 24½	...	12 12½	...	...	2 35½	3 12½	...	...	4 27½	...	...	7 32½	...	8 25	...	10 25
Seaton	11 29	.	12 17	.	*12 50*	2 40	3 17	.	.	4 32	.	.	7 37	.	8 30	.	10 30

UP	• a.m.		• a.m.		• N No.207 Empty p.m.		• p.m.	• p.m.		• p.m.		• p.m.		• p.m.		Excn. No.263 • L p.m.
Seaton ...	11 0	.	11 35	.	*12†25*	.	2 8	2 45	.	3 45	.	7 2	.	7 52	.	9 50
Colyford arr.	...	...	...	...	...	...	...	...	...	...	...	...	...	...	...	9 55
Colyford dep.	11 5	.	11 40	.	.	.	2 13	2 50	.	3 50	.	7 7	.	7 57	.	9 58
Colyton ...	11 9	...	11 44	...	...	...	2 17	2 54	...	3 54	...	7 11	...	8 1	...	10 2
Seaton Jct.	11 13	.	11 48	.	*12†35*	.	2 21	2 58	.	3 58	.	7 15	.	8 5	.	10 6

SUNDAYS COMMENCING 30th SEPTEMBER, 1951.

DOWN	• a.m.		• p.m.		• p.m.		• p.m.	
Seaton Jct. ...	11 17	.	12 5	.	2 55	.	4 20	.
Colyton ...	11 21½	...	12 9½	...	2 59½	...	4 24½	...
Colyford arr.	.	.	.	.	.	.	.	.
Colyford dep.	11 24½	...	12 12½	...	3 2½	...	4 27½	...
Seaton ...	11 29	.	12 17	.	3 7	.	4 32	.

UP	• a.m.		• a.m.		p.m.		• p.m.
Seaton ...	11 0	.	11 35	.	2 35	.	3 35
Colyford arr.	...	...	...	...	...	...	...
Colyford dep.	11 5	.	11 40	.	2 40	.	3 40
Colyton ...	11 9	...	11 44	...	2 44	...	3 44
Seaton Jct. ...	11 13	.	11 48	.	2 48	.	3 48

A—Will not apply when 1.53 p.m. Q Mixed runs.
C—Through coaches from Waterloo, until 8th September.
D—Work 10.10 a.m. from Seaton.
E—Runs as Mixed train when required.
F—Exmouth Jct. Engine.
G—Through coaches from Waterloo.
H—Through coaches to Waterloo.
J—Not to be held for 4.5 p.m. Q Waterloo.
L—Available for ordinary passengers.
M—Perform coaching shunting and assist 9.0 a.m. from Seaton.
N—Runs 24th June, 22nd July, 12th and 26th August and 9th September only.

The 18th June, 1951, Working Timetable for the branch.

At least during 1963, Warner's Holiday Camp, sited close to the station, each Monday and Friday organised a ramble beside the River Axe as far as the pub at Colyford. As this adjoined the station, the 12.01 pm from Seaton Junction might leave Colyford at 12.08 pm with several hundred passengers to Seaton.

The branch stations dealt with general merchandise and coal traffic, while additionally Seaton dealt with stone from the quarries at Beer; their revival (in February 1878) saw large quantities being sent to distant places. A small amount of fish traffic was carried, the opening of the railway enabling the catch to be marketed more quickly than previously. In later years, fish traffic was in the reverse direction, boxes being carried to Seaton in the guard's van of passenger trains. A six-wheeled goods guard's and cattle drovers' van No. 54962 (tare 17 tons 17 cwt.) was used as a brake van on the branch from the mid-1930s. It had a 26 ft long body containing a brake compartment, a saloon for drovers and a small section for storing forage. This van had previously worked on the Calstock branch. BR permitted passenger trains on the branch to be worked without a guard as long as the number of coaches did not exceed three.

One evening when the last train of the day arrived at Seaton, one of the passengers, a sailor, was found somewhat the worse for drink. When the porter called out, 'Seaton, all change', he became obstreperous and declared he would sit in the train until it arrived at Axmouth. The imaginative crew drew the train forward and reversed into the bay at Seaton. 'Axmouth, all change' they shouted and he stepped out contentedly.

COLYFORD.

Colyford station is staffed by one man, whose hours of attendance will be arranged by the Divisional Superintendent.

During the period when no member of the staff is on duty at Colyford, trains from Seaton Junction to Seaton must be brought to a stand at the home signal protecting Colyford level crossing. The Guard must then alight, proceed to the ground frame, place the gates across the road, and lower the home signal to admit the train to the platform. When the train has passed clear of the crossing the Guard must replace the down home signal to the Danger position, open the gates to the public, proceed to the platform, and after collecting the tickets of passengers alighting at Colyford and attending to the work of the train, give the Driver the All Right signal when the train is ready to leave. If the train is the last booked service to pass over the branch line for the day, the Guard must also extinguish any platform lamps that may be burning, but must leave the gate and signal lamps alight.

In the case of a train from Seaton to Seaton Junction, the Guard must, after the train has been brought to a stand at the platform, collect tickets from the passengers who alight, and attend to the work of the train. He must then proceed to the ground frame, place the gates across the road and lower the up starting signal. He must then give the Driver a hand signal to draw forward, and a further hand signal to stop when the train has passed clear of the crossing, after which he must replace the up starting signal to the Danger position, open the gates to the public, and, after joining the train, give the Driver an All Right signal.

The fares of all passengers joining up and down trains at Colyford during the period when no member of the staff is on duty at that place will be collected by the Guard.

Light engines are prohibited from running over the Seaton Branch during the time when the Porter is not in attendance at Colyford, unless they are accompanied by a member of the Traffic staff, who must attend to the opening and closing of the level crossing gates, as before mentioned.

An extract from the Western Section of the 1934, SR Working Timetable Appendices covering the working of Colyford station.

Chapter Four
Locomotives and Rolling Stock

Branch locomotives were stabled at Seaton. In the 1860s, Joseph Beattie's 2–2–2 well tanks of the 'Tartar' class, No. 12 *Jupiter* and No. 33 *Phoenix*, were working on the branch. By mid-1885 Beyer Peacock 0–6–0 'Ilfracombe Goods' engines Nos. 282 and 284 regularly ran on the line and in the 1890s the standard 2–4–0 well tank engines appeared. Then Adams '02' class 0–4–4 tank engine No. 213 (built in 1892) became the branch engine and remained until transferred in mid-1914.

'S14' class 0–4–0 motor tank engines were tried on the branch c.1911, but were unsuccessful and their coal consumption was little better than a locomotive of the '02' class.

From 1913 onwards, one of the Lyme Regis branch 4–4–2Ts (when spare) could be seen on the Seaton branch, while in the early years of Grouping, motor-fitted No. 0486 relieved the '02' class on the Seaton branch until it was withdrawn in January 1928. In June 1914 '02' class 0–4–4T Nos. 201 and 204, which had been modified with mechanical gear for motor working, were sent to Seaton. (No. 201 later became W34 *Newport* and worked on the Isle of Wight.)

In the mid-1920s motor-fitted '02' class Nos. 183 and 236 worked the Seaton branch. Although the Ministry of Transport expressed concern regarding the inefficiency of the manual control gear, it was not replaced until a series of potentially dangerous incidents on the Bournemouth West, Wimborne and Brockenhurst line in 1929–1930 caused SR officials to ban its use.

Following the successful trial on 29th January, 1930 of ex-LBSCR Stroudley 'D1' class 0–4–2T No B234, regular working by this class started on 19th June. They had been displaced by electric working in the London area and worked the Seaton branch with Brighton two-coach motor sets fitted for air control push-pull operation, the engine usually propelling the train to Seaton. In 1932 the 'D1s' working the services were Nos. B214 and B256, together with Adams '02' No. E182, Drummond 'M7' 0–4–4 tank No. E45 and Drummond 'L11' 4–4–0 No. E167. 'T9' 4–4–0s appeared on excursions. In the 1930s, several engines of the '02' class were fitted with compressed air gear for working push-pull trains, a donkey pump being attached to the left-hand side of the smokebox with the reservoir immediately below on the running plate. No. 187, which had been so fitted in November 1932, and Nos. 183 and 207 in September 1933 were shedded at Exmouth Junction for working trains on the Seaton branch.

'M7' class 0–4–4Ts were also converted for air operation of motor trains, No. 45 being transferred to Exmouth Junction for the Seaton branch in October 1932. 'M7' No. 27 was seen on this duty on 14th July, 1936 while in mid-1937 Nos. 27, 46 and 55 were similarly noted.

'M7s' Nos. 46, 49, 55, and 105 were on the branch in the latter period of SR ownership, and in BR times Nos. 30021, 30045, 30046, 30048, 30105 and 30480 appeared; 'M7' working ceased in early May 1963. On at least one

Ex-LBSCR 'D1' class 0–4–2T No. B256 and gated saloons (probably Set 373) at the branch platform, Seaton Junction in the early nineteen-thirties. *Lens of Sutton*

A fine side view of Adams 4–4–2T No. 3488 at Seaton Junction on Saturday 9th July, 1949. *H.C. Casserley*

No. 30021 alongside the Express Dairy Milk and Egg Depot at Seaton Junction on 15th July, 1958. *H.C. Casserley*

Saturday in 1947 the Devon Belle with 14 Pullmans was stopped by signals at the foot of Honiton Bank, a gradient of 1 in 80, could not restart, and had to wait for an 'M7' to come from the Seaton branch and assist as pilot.

The 'M7s' were not displaced on the Seaton branch by BR Standard class '3MT' 2-6-2Ts or Ivatt class '2MTs', because push-and-pull engines were required.

SR engines prohibited from running over the branch were:

4-6-2	'Merchant Navy', 'West Country' and 'Battle of Britain'
4-6-0	'H15'; 'N15'; 'N15X'; 'T14'
2-6-0	'N'; 'U'
4-4-0	'D15'; 'B4X'
2-6-4T	'W'

0-6-0 locomotives of the Maunsell 'Q' class, Bulleid 'Q1' class and diesel shunters Nos. 15211-36 (though not the ex-SR shunters Nos. 15201-3) were passed to work on the branch, as also were Eastern Region Thompson 'B1' 4-6-0s and BR Standard 'Clan' class Pacifics, the last two types subject to a limit of 40 mph, but it is doubtful whether representatives of any of these classes actually worked on the line. BR Standard '3MT' 2-6-2 tank engine No. 82040 also appeared. With the removal of restrictions in 1960, Ashford Moguls and light Pacifics were permitted to run on the branch, 'U' class engines Nos. 31792, 31798 and 'West Country' No. 34030 *Watersmeet* being noted in 1963. No. 21C120 *Seaton* was named at a ceremony at Seaton Junction on 25th June, 1946.

On 2nd May, 1963 No. 30048 and a three-coach motor set worked the branch for the last time, being relieved by WR 0-6-0PT No. 6400 and two trailer cars, the WR having gained control of the branch on 1st January, 1963. The other Pannier working the line was No. 6430, No. 6412 joining them in July for a while until all three were transferred to Yeovil when diesel multiple units arrived on the Seaton branch in November. The Panniers normally pushed the train of one auto coach to Seaton, but when taking the through coach from Waterloo, this, not being auto-fitted, had to be pulled, thus sandwiching the engine.

On 18th May, 1963 Ivatt class '2MT' 2-6-2T No. 41272 took over branch working and, as it was not equipped for auto-working, had to run round its train on each trip, leading to lateness when turnround times were tight. The Pannier tank reappeared a few days later, but again failed, No. 41309 working until 10th June when the Pannier tank recommenced duties.

The branch was dieselised on 4th November, 1963 and the multiple units were restricted to a maximum speed of 50 mph on the branch. On 26th September, 1964 a failed dmu was replaced by BR Standard class '3MT' 2-6-2T No. 82040 and a Mark 1 brake second coach. Owing to a series of dmu failures, ex-GWR 0-4-2 tank engines Nos. 1442 and 1450, borrowed from Yeovil shed, travelled to Seaton on Sunday 7th February, 1965, No. 1442 then normally working the branch trains and No. 1450 being held as a stand-by. The dmus took over again after about a month. Both engines were put in store on 11th May, 1965. No. 1442 is now preserved at Tiverton and No. 1450 on the Dart Valley Railway.

In the steam era, on weekdays a BR Standard class '3' or Ivatt class '2' 2−6−2 tank engine often worked the 4.30 am Exmouth Junction−Seaton freight, but on Saturdays an 0−4−4 tank engine was rostered as it became the branch engine for the following week. On summer Saturdays the two engines shared branch duties until the last through train arrived, when the retiring engine travelled to Exmouth Junction shed either light, or piloting the 3.46 pm stopping passenger from Seaton Junction to Exeter, where it received a boiler washout and other maintenance. In winter months the retiring engine worked to Exeter on the freight.

At various periods some Saturday trains on the branch were double-headed, either to work back engines, or because of heavy loads. In 1959 two of the Adams 4−4−2 tank engines double-headed a weed-killing train.

From 1st January, 1892 the locomotive headcode for the Seaton branch was one lamp or disc to the right of the smoke box when viewed head-on; then from 1st May, 1901 there was a disc on the left of the smokebox and a diamond to the right. In 1921 when diamonds were abolished, the branch reverted to a disc to the right of the smoke box, this lasting until the end of Southern Region steam.

Four-wheeled coaches would have been in use from opening up to about 1910, when six-wheeled stock appeared briefly before bogie push-pull units arrived. 'Gated' LSWR 2-coach push-pull sets Nos. 363, 373 and 374 were used and consisted of a third class coach plus a driver-brake composite coach. They were unsuited to visitors; when the two streams of disembarking passengers laden with luggage crowded into the central vestibule, only when they reached the gate did they discover that it opened inwards!

From 1916 to c.1924, No. 72, a converted Eagle Express saloon fitted with end gangways, strengthened the branch train when required. As it was 8 ft 0¾ in. in width, compared with 8 ft 6 in. of the branch set, and as it was the practice at that time for a strengthening coach to be placed in the centre of the train and left there for the whole of the summer season, the appearance of the set was ruined.

For a brief period in the late 1940s, two short-bodied ex-LSWR sets Nos. 734 and 735, comprising composites Nos. 4759 and 4760 and control vehicles Nos. 2644 and 2655, appeared. Converted for push-pull working in 1943, they had originally been built for use on the Channel Islands boat trains.

In 1949, some of the 'Ironclad' coaches which had served the branch on through trains were converted to push-pull working: Set 381 consisting of control vehicle No. 4052 and composite No. 6560 and similarly Set 385 with No. 3213 and No. 6564. Reconstruction was quite extensive, lavatories being altered into coupés, and the brake thirds had a control vestibule fitted and another compartment added in what had previously been luggage space. The corridor connections were removed.

In the early 1950s, ex-LBSCR low, arc-roofed coaches appeared. Set 723 comprised of No. 3855, a 6-compartment brake control vehicle, and 9-compartment composite (two first and seven third) No. 6250.

Ex-SECR No. 1064, a 10-compartment third was kept at Seaton Junction for strengthening the branch set, but from October 1957 was paired with No. 6488 in Set 1, replacing ex-LSWR No. 2620. Another interesting strengthening vehicle in the 1950s was No. 1050. It appeared from Lancing Works in 1927 consisting of five compartments from an ex-SECR second class 6-wheeler, three compartments from a similar third class vehicle, and two compartments of uncertain origin. It worked on Eastern Section lines until 1943 when it was downgraded to all-third and fitted with the necessary compressed air pipes for push-pull working.

From c.1960, BR converted Maunsell stock into Sets 603 and 616, with composite brake control No. 6675 and No. 6695, and open second No. 1320 and No. 1358 respectively, the latter being replaced by No. 1359 in November 1961. These sets were the last steam conversions to push-pull working on BR.

Although the branch engine normally had only two, or three coaches, at holiday periods it had, on occasions, to start seven, or even eight coaches up the gradient of 1 in 76 from Colyton. In the early 1950s Sunday trains were reduced to just one coach.

In the 1960s sets Nos. 1, 31 and 878 were also used together with Western Region auto coaches Nos. 235, 238, 240 and 253.

An ex-LMS, 12-wheeled coach, labelled 'Motive Power Department Seaton' on an isolated length of track at Seaton on 8th September, 1953.   *S.W. Baker*

A Gloucester Railway Carriage & Wagon Company single car dmu stands in 1964, at Platform 2. Note the engine shed and coal stage on the left.   *Lens of Sutton*

The same Gloucester single car dmu approaches Colyford on a down working in 1964.   *Lens of Sutton*

Coach 564725 at Seaton Junction on 24th September, 1956. This vehicle was a LSWR, 56′ brake lavatory composite coach built at Eastleigh in December 1903 and withdrawn in October 1956.   *R.H. Casserley*

A brake and cattle drovers van seen here at Seaton on 12th March, 1952.   *A.E. West*

Car No. 8 *en route* from Seaton terminus and passing in front of the depot gates on 4th April, 1989. *Author*

Cars Nos. 12 and 6 in the depot yard with No. 12's bogies removed for maintenance on 4th April, 1989. *Author*

Chapter Five
The Seaton Tramway

Modern Electric Tramways Ltd, formed in May 1953, operated narrow gauge double-deck tramcars, two-thirds the size of their British prototypes, on a track at the Crumbles, Eastbourne and towards the end of the tenure of its site there, Claude W. Lane, the Managing Director and Engineer searched for a new location. He believed that the then threatened Seaton branch held possibilities, visited Paddington and five years of negotiations ensued. His was not the only scheme hoping to resurrect the line, S.C. Pritchard of Peco model railway fame hoped to take over the Seaton branch, as well as the disused track of the singled main line between Seaton Junction and Axminster, and also the Lyme Regis branch, thus giving him the possibility of through running from Seaton to Lyme Regis. British Railways rejected this suggestion as it did not wish to encourage parallel competition.

Following closure of the Seaton branch, Modern Electric Tramways Ltd obtained an option on the three miles of track bed from Seaton to Colyton; the remaining 1¾ miles to the former Seaton Junction were not required as they had no traffic potential, since the main line railhead had been transferred to Axminster. The section from Colyton to the junction was purchased by farmers who owned adjacent property.

At an inquiry at Seaton Town Hall on 19th November, 1969 conducted by K.A.S. Phillips for the Ministry of Transport, Modern Electric Tramways Ltd applied for an order transferring to them the rights to operate a light railway. This was granted as the Seaton & Beer Transfer Order 1970 (Statutory Instruments No. 34). Permission had already been granted to the British Railways Board in the BRB (Seaton & Beer) Light Railway Order, (Statutory Instruments No. 835) on 18th June, 1969.

Ninety Colyton residents, concerned that the natural beauties of the Axe Valley would be disturbed, objected to the tramway. The Chief Constable of Devon & Cornwall suggested that no more than six trams an hour should use the level crossing at Colyford, and no trams be run in pairs. The tramway project had the support of Devon County Council, Seaton Urban District Council and the Seaton Chamber of Trade, all these bodies realising that the tramway would become a tourist attraction as well as providing local transport. The Ministry of Transport granted the application since it saw that restoring the line would be in no way detrimental to the Axe Valley.

The last tram ran at Eastbourne on 14th September, 1969 and in February 1970 the job of transporting the equipment to Seaton started. Claude Lane and his assistant Allan Gardner made 36 return journeys with two lorries, one often towing a trailer, moving the nine cars, track, a workshop, generating engines, dynamos, batteries, 160 traction poles, overhead equipment and tons of stores. A contract had been placed with Messrs Tyler of Tonbridge for an asbestos-clad building 105 ft by 45 ft to serve as a four-road tram depot, generating station, workshop and office.

Track laying began at Seaton early in 1970 and by midsummer the 2 ft 9 in. gauge single track extended as far as Bobsworth Bridge, so called

The Seaton Tramway garter crest as used on the side panels of the tramcars. *Author*

The tramway logo as seen at Colyton station. *Author*

The underbridge south of Colyton station photographed in 1989 with the 'Kerslake Exeter' builders cast name still visible. *Author*

Notice to tram drivers at Colyford level crossing. *Author*

The tea rooms at Colyton which have been tastefully adapted for the Seaton tramway from the original station buildings. As seen in April 1989. *Author*

A view in April 1989, looking towards the end of the tramway at Colyton station. *Author*

The tramway at Colyford station looking north with the generator hut on the left.
Author

Car No. 8 bound for Seaton terminus leaving Colyford station on 4th April, 1989.
Author

Bogie-truck seen here in the depot at Seaton (*above*).
Author

A set of spring points at Colyford station (*right*).
Author

The treadle seen here at Colyford station which, when triggered by the tramcar wheel flanges, cancels the red level crossing signals (*left*).
Author

The old SR lengthsmen's hut, now the Seaton tramways generator hut, just north of Colyford level crossing (*right*).
Author

because the return fare to this terminus was a shilling. The 30 lb./yd rail was carried on ex-BR sleepers sawn into half lengths and the existing former railway ballast used. Following inspection by Lt Col Townsend Rose of the Railway Inspectorate on 27th May, 1970, the tram service began at 2.30 pm on 28th August and, as the overhead was not ready, power for car No. 8 was obtained from a battery trailer. This subsidiary of Modern Electric Tramways was known as the Seaton & District Electric Tramway Company.

During the winter of 1970–1 the main timbers of Bobsworth Bridge were renewed and the track extended to south of Colyford level crossing. It was found that the new rails fractured in use and the whole line was re-laid with stronger 30 lb./yd flat-bottom rails recovered from a closed section of the Sierra Leone Government Railway. In 1972 the track was welded into 60 ft lengths. Passing loops were provided at Seaton Riverside, Axmouth loop (½ mile to the north) and Swan's Nest loop, north of Bobsworth Bridge.

Following the death of Claude Lane on 2nd April, 1971, his post was filled by his chief assistant, Allan Gardner. The battery-powered service between Seaton Riverside and Colyford recommenced on 9th April, 1971. The erection of green traction poles set at intervals of 40 yds was completed early in 1973 and the ⅜ in. overhead wire strung that summer. The majority of overhead fittings – hangers, ears, frogs and insulators – were purchased from Bradford Corporation when its trolley bus system was being dismantled. Other overhead fittings – trolley arms, bases and heads – were purchased from Hamburg City Tramways following its closure on 1st October, 1978. The first time a car received power from the overhead, rather than a battery trailer, was on 23rd September, 1973.

In 1974 a ½ mile-long extension was built down a gradient of 1 in 40 to a much more accessible terminus at the central car park in Harbour Road. This involved crossing marshy land a little above sea level. A thousand tons of brick rubble was obtained from a local brickworks to form a solid track bed. Two bridges were built across dykes using reinforced concrete plinths supporting steel transverse beams. As this section had several 90 degree curves with somewhat limited viewing, to prevent cars colliding head-on a token was required to be carried. This section opened on 17th May, 1975, boosting the number of passengers carried that season to 36,000.

At 11.30 pm on 15th November, 1975, BR 90 lb./yd rail was removed from the level crossing over the A3052 (formerly the A35) road at Colyford and replaced with (ex-Sheffield Corporation) grooved tram rail at 2 ft 9 in. gauge, the road being reinstated by 8 am. Although the line onwards to Colyton was mostly completed by 1978, construction during the winter of 1979 of a new flood relief scheme by the South West Water Authority, immediately adjacent to the level crossing, delayed the installation of traffic lights until that autumn. Following a Ministry of Transport inspection on 3rd March, 1980, the tramway was extended to Colyton five days later. The procedure introduced for a tram wishing to cross is as follows:

When a tram driver is ready to go over the level crossing, he must draw his car up to the stop board and, as an act of courtesy to other road users, the managing director, Allan Gardner, has instructed tram drivers if possible to

The unique mobile shop No. 01 seen here coupled to outside power at Seaton terminus in April 1989. *Author*

A very sharp curve from Seaton depot, looking towards the car park with the holiday camp on the left. *Author*

wait for a lull in the road traffic, before pressing the plunger. This operation activates a circuit, an amber light shows to road traffic for eight seconds, after which the red flashing lamps remain on until the first set of tramcar wheels passes over a track-mounted treadle on the opposite side of the crossing. As the track on the south side is double, the Ministry of Transport required a treadle on each line to cover the eventuality of wrong road running.

The extension opened up a completely different vista as the rural scenery north of the crossing was a complete contrast to the estuarine scenery to the south. The tramway caused more visitors to experience the delights of Colyton and this led to certain problems. In 1980 the *Seaton News* in connection with a parish council meeting at Colyton reported: 'The council should write back to say the tram company should provide toilets and also point out that the flow of passengers was not seasonal . . . but all the year round.'

Today power is taken from South Western Electricity Board mains at Seaton and Colyton, diesel generators and traction batteries augmenting the 440 volt dc supply. Both generators were manufactured by Messrs R.A. Lister of Dursley, Gloucestershire, one of 6 hp being sited just north of Colyford level crossing and one of 7½ hp just south of Bobsworth Bridge. Both are housed in former Southern Railway lengthmen's huts. A member of the depot staff fills the fuel tanks, lubricates and turns the generators on. Points and overhead switches are sprung to give left-hand running through loops, though at Seaton Riverside, by the depot, the right-hand loop is used to avoid a car climbing a stiff gradient and taking a sharp left curve which would be likely to induce wheel spin.

The tramway employs five full-time staff and these are assisted by 97 part-time volunteers. The line is open daily from Easter until the end of November, and Mondays to Fridays from December till Easter. About 200 local people hold season tickets. Visitors at the two holiday camps near the tramway terminus at Seaton provide a steady source of traffic, many taking the opportunity of an enjoyable tram ride. The system grows busier each year, about 79,000 passengers using the tramway in 1988.

Appendix One

LSWR statistics inspected by H. Cecil Newton on behalf of the Seaton & Beer Railway

Goods and Mineral traffic carried on the SBR in the 6 months ending 30th June, 1876

	Carted tons	Not Carted tons	Coals & Minerals tons	Total tons
Jan.	92	236	71	399
Feb.	82	171	191	444
Mar.	91	671	129	891
Apr.	110	552	111	773
May	89	208	211	508
June	76	244	448	768
	540	2082	1161	3783

Estimate of terminals on above:

2622 tons at 1s. 6d. ton	£196 13s. 0d.
1161 tons at 9d. ton	£ 43 10s. 9d.
	£240 3s. 9d.

Statement of Railway Clearing House on traffic between SBR and stations beyond LSWR for half year ending 30th June, 1876

	Carted & Not Carted tons	Minerals tons	Coals tons	Total tons
Colyton	696	165	146	1007
Seaton	264	115	188	567
	960	280	334	1574

Through Coal Traffic (tons)

	Via Templecombe	Via Yeovil
Colyton	132	590
Seaton	230	829

Railway Clearing House division of above with the LSWR

		Mileage	Terminals	Total
Colyton:	General goods	£30 1s. 0d.	£51 0s. 8d.	£81 1s. 8d.
	Coal & mineral	£18 14s. 10d.	£8 12s. 3d.	£27 7s. 1d.
Seaton:	General goods	£52 7s. 5d.	£20 17s. 7d.	£73 5s. 0d.
	Coal & mineral	£60 6s. 2d.	£8 3s. 6d.	£68 9s. 8d.

Outwards traffic between all stations on the SBR and LSWR

Year	1873	1874	1875	1876
	Tons	Tons	Tons	Tons
Jan.	NA	1935	2028	2377
Feb.	NA	1662	1679	3287
Mar.	NA	1901	2286	2401
Apr.	NA	2772	2738	2904
May	NA	3231	3338	3235
June	NA	3316	3239	4286
July	4349	4745	4442	5415
Aug.	4215	4436	4825	NA
Sept.	3606	3843	4211	NA
Oct.	2877	3040	2888	NA
Nov.	1896	2086	2065	NA
Dec.	2159	2051	2412	NA

October 1876 passengers booked from the SBR to the LSWR
(the number of passengers booked beyond the LSWR was very small)

Class	1	2	3	Parliamentary	Total
Colyton Town					
Single	13	23	–	1077	1113
Return	7	15	5		27
Colyford					
Single	12	11	–	657	680
Return	2	8	5		15
Seaton					
Single	33	62	–	1041	1136
Return	43	45	14		102

Fares		Single			Return	
	1	2	3		1	2
Seaton Jc & Colyton Town	4d.	3d.	1½d.		7d.	5d.
Colyford	7	5	2½		1.0	9
Seaton	11	8	4		1.8	1.2
Colyton Town & Colyford	3	2	1		5	4
Seaton	6	4	2½		10	7
Colyford & Seaton	4	3	1½		7	5

SBR Share of Income from goods traffic for the 6 months ending 31st December, 1876

	General goods	Coal & mineral	Livestock	Total
Colyton	£27 4s. 2d.	£21 18s. 4d.		£49 2s. 6d.
Terminal	£53 5s. 11d.	£11 13s. 10d.		£64 19s. 9d.
Seaton	£49 6s. 0d.	£41 2s. 2d.	£0 3s. 7d.	£90 11s. 9d.
Terminal	£14 15s. 8d.	£8 16s. 6d.		£23 12s. 2d.
Light traffic	8s. 3d.			8s. 3d.
	£145 0s. 0d.	£83 10s. 10d.	£0 3s. 7d.	£228 14s. 5d.

Notes

Traffic from SBR to LSWR divided by mileage proportion, no terminal allowed. Traffic SBR to beyond the LSWR, including the Somerset & Dorset Railway (i.e. Railway Clearing House traffic), mileage proportion plus terminal, a special terminal being paid on coal. RCH terminals: 4 shillings on carted; 1s. 6d. on non-carted and 9d. a ton on coal. Carting agent paid 2s. 6d. a ton for collection and delivery, so the net terminal was 1s. 6d. ton.

Tonnages during the half year ending 30th June, 1877

	Tons
Local traffic	3420
'Foreign' RCH traffic	1627
Through coal traffic	1500
	6547

Statistics for the half year ending 31st December, 1877

	Tons
Local traffic	3337
'Foreign' RCH traffic	2523
Through coal traffic	1521
	7381

Number of passengers: approximately 47,000.

	SBR	Buckfastleigh Rly
Average yield for goods traffic	9d.	1s. 8d.
Average yield for passenger traffic	4d.	7d.

A Bank Holiday return excursion leaving Seaton on 6th August, 1934 as seen from the far side of the River Axe. The train is headed by 'L11' class 4–4–0 No. 154 hauling nine six-wheeled coaches.   *S.W. Baker*

Appendix Two
Station Statistics

	Colyton			Colyford			Seaton		
	1928	1932	1936	1928	1932	1936	1928	1932	1936
No. passenger tickets issued	19814	16683	13431	4698	2861	2385	25059	15490	13471
No. season tickets issued	23	106	54	–	6	6	60	166	183
No. platform tickets issued	303	28	16	–	–	–	2999	1600	2260
Parcels forwarded	1099	1180	1097	288	148	269	3401	2524	2412
Parcels received	5553	5274	6036	616	484	493	20582	20055	21994
Horses forwarded	–	1	–	–	–	–	7	4	5
Horses received	–	–	–	–	–	–	9	7	2
Milk forwarded (churns 1928, gallons 1932 & 1936)	4226	43750	–	579	17594	2126	96	–	3923
Milk received "	13	248	–	–	17	–	353	1039	3753
General merchandise forwarded (tons)	626	363	265	–	–	–	668	413	423
General merchandise received (tons)	4015	3570	3864	–	–	–	2746	2062	1929
Coal, coke, patent fuel, forwarded (tons)	–	–	–	–	–	–	26	65	18
Coal, coke, patent fuel, received (tons)	2712	3005	2736	–	–	–	5007	6073	5832
Other minerals forwarded (tons)	4	6	–	–	–	–	629	263	65
Other minerals received (tons)	3282	421	174	–	–	–	4582	1129	1095
Livestock forwarded (no. of trucks)	26	18	14	–	–	–	8	3	3
Livestock received "	11	6	1	–	–	–	106	75	16

Notes:
Holiday camp opened at Seaton in 1935.
Decrease in lavatory receipts at Seaton from £17 6s. 0d. 1931, to £8 7s. 0d. 1932, owing to shop opposite station having a lavatory built towards the end of 1931 for use of own staff and public, both of whom used station facilities previously.

London and South Western Ry.
787
From WATERLOO
TO
COLYFORD

Appendix Three

Extract from the Appendix to the Book of Rules and Regulations, 1st January, 1911

Special Instructions for Seaton Line
During certain portions of the year, this line is worked by a small type of engine and the loads of trains must be arranged as follows:

Maximum Loads, Seaton Junction to Seaton

Passenger trains	Equal to 40 wheels, including brake vehicles
Mixed trains	Equal to 52 wheels, the passenger stock on a train not to exceed 24 wheels
Goods trains	13 wagons and 1 van

Maximum Loads, Seaton to Seaton Junction

Passenger trains	Equal to 40 wheels, including brake vehicles
Mixed trains	Equal to 40 wheels, the passenger stock on a train not to exceed 24 wheels
Goods trains	11 wagons and 1 van to Colyton
	10 wagons and 1 van Colyton to Seaton Junction

Appendix Four

Fleet List of Rolling Stock on The Seaton Tramway

WORKS VEHICLES

No.	Date Built	Type	Other Information
01	1954	Mobile Shop	Built as Boat Car; converted to Works Car in 1960 and Mobile Shop 1965.
02	1969	Works Car	
03	1986	Bogie Wagon	
04	1987	Hoist Wagon	
05	1988	4 Wheel Truck	
–		Side Tipper	
–	1959	Ruston & Hornsby	4-wheel diesel locomotive Class 48DL, maker's No. 435398. Arrived Seaton c.September 1972. Purchased from North Devon Clay Co. Ltd., Peters Marland, North Devon.

PASSENGER CARRYING STOCK

No.	Date Built	No. of Seats	Type
2	1964	35	Open top double decker based on Metropolitan Electric Tramways/London United Tramways design.
4	1961	20	Blackpool Boat type.
6	1955	37	Open top double decker, Bournemouth type.
7	1958	37	Open top double decker, Bournemouth type.
8	1968	41	Open top double decker, Bournemouth type. First ran 25th August, 1970.
12	1966	50	Single decker; converted to open top double decker 1980.
14	1904	27	Ex-Metropolitan Electric Tramways No. 94. Built by Brush Electrical Engineering Co. as an open top double decker. Ran on routes in North London. Top cover added 1929; withdrawn 1935; sold to Mr Cross of Upshire, near Waltham Cross. Removed to Eastbourne 1962 for preservation. Modern Electric Tramways rebuilt it as a single decker 1969, narrowing width by a foot to 5 ft 4 in. Designed to run at Eastbourne. Moved to Seaton November 1970.
16	1921	26	Ex-Bournemouth No. 106. Found at Kinson between Bournemouth and Wimborne. Narrowed to 5 ft 9 in.
17	1988	48	Toast rack, Manx Electric Railway type. Seats lift out so that it can carry 10/12 passengers in wheel chairs, plus 8 helpers.

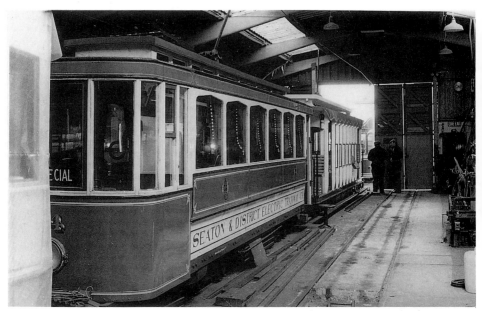

A final look at the Seaton Tramway with cars No. 14 and No. 17 at rest in the depot on 4th April, 1989.   *Author*